Rags of Time

Rags of Time

A Season in Prison

by Jack Cook

Beacon Press   Boston

This book is written for
and dedicated to
prisoners everywhere

Contents

Prologue

Having severed my connection with Selective Service while an instructor in English at Hobart and William Smith Colleges, Geneva, New York, in the spring of 1966, thereafter to join the peace movement as an editor of *The Catholic Worker*, a pacifist-anarchist monthly in New York City, I was indicted, tried, and convicted for Refusal To Be Inducted into the Armed Forces of the United States and sentenced to three years in prison on 4 January 1969 out of the Southern District Court, Foley Square, New York City, by Judge Metzner. After spending a week or so in the West Street Federal Detention Center in Manhattan, I was bussed, handcuffed to another prisoner, together with twenty-five other prisoners to Lewisburg Federal Penitentiary in Lewisburg, Pennsylvania. From there, after two weeks of the administration's and the inmate's orientation to prison life, I was sent to Allenwood Federal Prison Camp, located some fifteen miles away, an adjunct of the larger walled-in Lewisburg prison.

For me there was a beginning when I first heard Dorothy Day of *The Catholic Worker* at one of the Friday night meetings in the old Chrystie Street House of Hospitality on the Bowery, a place I soon came to love and hated to leave two years later when the community moved up to East First Street. She seemed weary. At that time she was sixty-eight and she spoke as if the end were near. (At seventy-two she still seems weary. But I know now her lurking gaiety. And she still speaks as if the end were near. But the slightest chore will put it off.) Yet in that summer of 1966, speaking and being heard as one with little time left, she thought it imperative to talk about Anarchy.

She turned her mind and, as it were, her face toward the

State; and, had it been there in that shabby room instead of us, it would have withered under that stare. No abstract ideology was forthcoming. She needed no mask to attend the Revolutionary Ball. Instead there were the anecdotes of governmental and corporate injustice she had seen over five decades and the stories of what this one and that one, names and nicknames, had done to alleviate the state-imposed pain. Direct, personal action; make the need of the oppressed your need; do for them, with them, what it would be impossible for them to do alone. No structure, no hierarchy, no formulated program; just people helping other people.

She reminded me of Emma Goldman, as my friend Dick Drinnon in his definitive biography presented her to his readers. Physically, she was as imposing as her predecessor; the same power, the same presence. And, like Emma, she offered the anarchism of Kropotkin, combined, though, not with the individualism of Ibsen, but with the mysticism and radical Christianity of Dostoevsky and Tolstoy.

Both women looked to a destructured, unauthoritarian society of equal individuals. "The individual is the heart of society," Emma said and Dorothy would certainly agree. Both envisioned "small organic organizations in free-cooperation with each other," as Dick Drinnon phrased it. But Dorothy was standing in, and could look back at, her dream and that of Peter Maurin (the co-founder of *The Catholic Worker*): a community within the shell of a larger community: the Houses of Hospitality that had, together with her newspaper, continued to survive, when other radical movements originating in the Thirties were but a memory or a travesty.

Both saw through, and the glance was indeed intrepid, the myths of the state, the corrosive manipulation of peoples, the repression and domination. Both looked upon liberal solutions, not conservativism's frantic gestures, as being the greater evil. Both turned indignant maternal glances on the budget of the Federal government that spends millions upon defense, so little on human needs. Both knew that real freedom must begin with personal freedom, internalized revolution, absolute conversion. Both incarnated Female Emancipation, Women's Liberation.

Both could look back, with bitterness, at a long series of lost causes, dashed hopes, disillusionments, and folly. For Emma there were Berkman jailed, a revolution caricatured, Sacco and Vanzetti, Berkman's suicide, the bloody executions, the defeat in Spain, repeated jailings, and the image of a "national bugaboo." For Dorothy there were the loss of old friends turned off by her pacifism during the Spanish Civil War, others turned liberal; the despair of the World War II period, when her stance further alienated her from leftists and her country-men; the loss of working class support, never to reappear even as the working class never quite reappeared after the war; con-stant misunderstanding and ridicule, publication debts, hassles with city government over housing regulations (she was once declared a slum landlord by a city judge) and with Federal government over nonpayment of taxes, repeated jailings, and the innumerable personal tragedies of the constantly growing, con-stantly dying community for which she was responsible.

Just as during a wet heavy snow, huge pine trees, their dark branches burdened with weight, take on increased stature and greater depth (a sculpture shadowed within, white without), even as the whole aspiring growth languishes—so did these two impassioned defenders of Folly and personal freedom carry into old age the weight of loss and long suffering.

Dorothy, perhaps even more than A. J. Muste and much before Martin Luther King, introduced into the American radical scene militant nonviolent direct action as a tactic with which to confront need and oppression. It was a weapon forged for her out of union struggles of the Twenties and Thirties, the Depression as it hit the Bowery, combined with the fearlessness of the slapped, perhaps, but not overcome radical Christian, and the teachings of Gandhi. Draft card burning, when that was declared a felony, began at the *Worker*. It was a Catholic Worker, Roger La Porte, whose immolation at the United Nations in 1966 threw New York City into its first (officially unexplained) blackout, and paralleled for us the sacrifice of the Buddhist monks of Saigon.

The face of Dorothy Day. The face of one who had descended over half a century ago to the very root of being, and, finding it, stayed—unlike so many honored others. The face of one so rooted in the core of the American and the radical experience, so close to the struggling men at the bottom, that through devotion and endurance, gentleness and solidarity, the heaping up of small things—bread and soup lines, rooms for the homeless, new old clothes, words of union, peace, and brotherhood—something high and great took form, bending around obstacles at the root ("When we need money, we pray for it"), and grew, imperceptibly, steadily, unhindered, and undeceived by the outward changes in the American scene. Something high and great, rooted in the squalor of the Lower East Side but penetrating into the very heavens. As the sole tree in the yard of Lewisburg prison absorbs all the dreams of every hung-up prisoner, his mind shattered on the street, as it yields to each prisoner's hopes as the seasons change and naked limbs are clothed in green; so did her compassion absorb the pain of men and women, borne by the time; so did her acceptance of this man's hunger, that woman's homelessness, make their needs her needs; so, too, was her yielding to the castoffs of a city empty of concern, of a government apathetic toward its own victims.

In that shabby soup kitchen on Chrystie Street, I saw flourishing the ideas closest to me—Anarchy, pacifism, radical Christianity. There, alive in the eyes of Dorothy Day, was "The Cretan Glance," as Kazantzakis wrote of it in his last work, *Report to Greco:*

> I gazed at the bullfights painted on the walls: the woman's agility and grace, the man's unerring strength, how they played with the frenzied bull, confronting him with intrepid glances. They did not kill him out of love in order to unite with him, as in oriental religions, or because they were overcome with fear and dared not look at him. Instead, they played with him, obstinately, respectfully, without hate. Perhaps even with gratitude. For this sacred battle with the bull whetted the Cretan's strength, cultivated his bodily agility and grace, the fiery yet coolheaded precision of movement, the discipline of will, the valor—so difficult to acquire—to measure his strength against the beast's fear-

ful power without being overcome by panic. Thus the Cretans transubstantiated horror, turning it into an exalted game in which man's virtue, in direct contact with mindless omnipotence, received stimulation and conquered—conquered without annihilating the bull, because it considered him not an enemy but a fellow worker. Without him, the body would not have become so flexible and strong, the soul so valiant.

Surely a person needs great training of both body and soul if he is to have the endurance to view the beast and play such a dangerous game. But once he is trained and acquires the feel of the game, every one of his movements becomes simple, certain, and leisurely; he looks upon fear with intrepidity.

As I regarded the battle depicted on the walls, the age-old battle between man and bull (whom today we term God), I said to myself, Such was the Cretan Glance.

Such are Dorothy's agility and grace, her unerring strength, after seven decades on this earth, that her movement of fellow workers, after thirty-eight years on the Lower East Side, still flourishes, still serves, still attracts the gentle faces, torn psyches, the souls hurting from a love they cannot handle; so they ladle soup instead for the uneasy faces, give out clean clothes for rags, and soothe for a time their own and another's torn psyche with love in a hectic home.

I followed my kind to the Bowery. Not the young peace people only, nor the draft resisters (though I was one of them), nor the liberal well-wishers (I was partly that, too); but I followed the Bowery men, my kind: the lost, jobless, sick and lonely, empty and roleless men of the insane Sixties, Fifties, Forties, and Thirties. The children of the Depression; the babies of the Bomb. Men in whom not even the memory of the recollection of the dream of what America might have been—not even *that* survived.

I went to *The Catholic Worker* because it was necessary for me to begin at the beginning. The Bowery is an end. The last ditch. The Gutter of Gutters for hopeless men this whole land wide; yet it is a beginning, too. Where else but at the bottom, after all? When everyone else seemed devoted to making a living, deliberate distraction in spite of the abyss, it was necessary to go where that kind of life had stopped; it was necessary in order to find out what living was all about.

At the beginning, then: Poverty—make it voluntary, yet conniving, a hustle; Community—color it chaotic, demanding, devastating, lonely; Service—label it haughty when not impatient, sometimes disturbing, poignant; Squalor—bedbugs, lice, tedium, despair; Pacifism—see it manhandle or be beaten by drunks and druggies, curse the idlers, "sit down" for hours upon hours, get arrested, and arrested; Anarchy—no law from above, Dorothy, not yours, not the churches', not the State's; Unionism—the gentle-shrewd Chavez; Propaganda of the Word, Anarchy of the Deed—articles written in haste before deadlines (Dorothy's need) when that overshadowed every other need, speeches, teach-ins, picketing, and marches; Marriage—a union celebrated in the soup kitchen one week before my imprisonment; Celebration—making love in a sleeping bag on a tenement rooftop, drinking with Bowery men, men soon to become Bowery men, with friends; Death—walk with it, talk with it, sleep with it, feed it, clothe it, look at it in the mirror, at the morgue identify it, watch it play around garbage cans, sleep in hallways, shatter into a thousand glittering bloodstained pieces of glass, watch it put Bowery men in Paddy Wagons; Resistance—"I am proud to plead guilty to this charge. To hell with the arrogance of the State!"; Need—for endurance, for flesh to touch flesh, spirit, spirit; for knowledge to make connections, to push a truth through the darkness; to withdraw, at times, from understanding as from "the gulfs their slimed foundations bared"—to be and to be not.

The narration that follows concerns events that took place at the Allenwood and Lewisburg prisons during less than a two-week period in the spring of 1970—one year or more into my "time" in jail, and in the tenth year of our involvement in the Southeast Asian War.

The narrative does not purport to tell the whole story of my confinement or, for that matter, of the conditions of life within the prisons of this country. My "official" sentence began in January of 1969. It ended twenty-three months later in November of 1970. I was released by court order, my sentence and conviction vacated, as a result of the Supreme Court decision that held that local draft boards acted unconstitutionally when they punitively reclassified and ordered up for induction those who protested against the War in Vietnam by returning their cards to the local boards.

Prisoners, as well as soldiers, talk endlessly of doing their "time." The months, days, and hours are counted and recorded. But having been a prisoner rather than a soldier, it is clear to me now, as it must be to all soldiers, that "time," "prison," "the service," and "the street" are truly relative terms. Each of us, either inside or outside a prison, does his own time, makes his own prison—regardless really of the institutions or the moment in which we happen to be living. This is the story, then, of a moment in my time. I offer it simply in hopes that it may help someone do his time, even "Good time" I hope.

Spring

Springtime in prison, Springtime in a "showplace" prison in these ununited States of America, who can imagine it? Spring is a time as unreal to those who have felt it as an evening in a cell is . . . unimaginable to those who have not been there. Nor is there a way out: flowers, blue and yellow, must bloom even in the fields of a prison camp, and Spring in a prisoner's head is, indeed, a strange season.

One of the first signs of Spring in prison is the shedding of coats. In the corridors, the corners, on the porches of dormitories, in the garbage cans and trash barrels, the brown and black bundles of discarded prison-issued coats are seen. Pea jackets, stolen from "Old Industries"—the name of a dilapidated structure once used as a factory for prison labor—by score-seeking inmates, or secured only after much conniving months ago with clothing-exchange inmates and, perhaps, paid for with a "box" (carton) of cigarettes, are thrown away with as much abandon as the regular issue coat, those made by inmates in their joint's industries for inmates in every other joint. It is a brown, two-pocketed, blue-buttoned jacket with a string running through it which, when tied inside at the belly, tended then to give some shape to an otherwise shapeless, always overly large Troll's coat, whose bulk was perhaps conceived with contraband in mind. For, all through Spring, some men still carried coats to and from the mess hall, on long walks in warm weather, and their function then, as always, was to hide what was being toted away.

I walked all winter long my second winter in jail in a pea-green tundra coat, the ragged edge of which reached below my knees; the shaggy red lining of the hood covered all but my nose. The only one of its kind in camp, it was designed for use by the cattle crew, who work with silage and in unheated barns during some extremely cold periods. Dan, a friend and fellow *Catholic Worker*-type, then on the cattle crew of the Allenwood farm, gave it to me. The coat fitted so well one of my nicknames that it became known to the population at large as "the Red Bear's coat." Part of my delight in it was that, ragged, patched, and unsightly as it was, it was never in danger of being stolen. So I'd leave it almost standing by itself in the corner of the hallway at the entrance to the mess hall and not worry about its being gone when I returned. Once, when it did appear that it was stolen, my uptight hard-core friends sent out the word that a pipe was waiting for the head of the guy found wearing it. It turned out that one of my hard-core friends, a young Italian with whom I lifted weights, lifted my coat just to see what changes it would put me through. Strangely enough, such sadistic pleasure at a buddy's expense is considered a mark of affection, especially among younger Mafia types. To create an emotion in another is a vital act, for the typical response to those not of one's group, nor a partner, is varying degrees of the "freeze." But I did not shed my old, tattered coat; it was shredded, officially, for me by order of the superintendent of the camp, who had perhaps heard how I was jailing on it. After it was confiscated and ripped up by the hack (a "screw" in time past, a "correctional officer" according to present usage) in charge of quarters, I was issued the regular fare. But by that time it was almost Spring.

And Spring comes with renewed activity: crows in long, winding black ribbons fly from field to field, no longer scavenging in ones and twos around the dorms as they do in winter; on branches of trees and bushes the unopened little balls of Spring dance in a green breeze; and the fields that border the compound heave the bind of snow and ice, and, warmed by the healing sun, release the long-confined hordes of wild flowers and extravagant weeds, as suddenly as the Lewisburg inmates, all winter long kept inside the prison buildings, break forth in Spring into the prison yard for recreation.

The inmates of Allenwood, too, minimum security types (tax evaders, "draft dodgers," druggies of all sorts, embezzlers, paperhangers, and such), as well as "short-timers" (men who have done all but a few months, or with perhaps a year or two left on long bits for bank robbery, murder, rape, etc.), who literally confine themselves, who must construct bars within their heads for lack of bars physically to grasp—these inmates move in Spring in ever-increasing numbers out of their "homes" in the dormitories into the air of this valley, as they were free to do all winter long, and onto the road that runs behind the two new brick dorms and between the dorms and Penny Hill, the eastern boundary of the prison compound. The road then runs in a long horseshoe curve, pasture and wood beyond on the left, the softball field, handball, and bocci ball courts within the horseshoe; and, curving again, it puts the Education Building (where I taught), the powerhouse, the "Palace" (weight-lifting gym), and garage for the fire engine on the left, while it intersects the road leading up to Project I (a new and absurdly grotesque Administration building underway, designed with at least eighteen different angular sides to it), and the old clapboard, Navy-barrack-type administration structure at the top of the hill in a direct line with the new dorms to its right.

The oldest dorm, called Number 5 or "The Jungle," rat-infested, dreary, a firetrap, and beyond repair (but actually preferred as living quarters by Mafia and other cliques, including some C.O.'s) straddles the hill beyond which the two dorms, flat brick buildings, as inoffensive as new grade schools, and as identical as Tweedle-Dum and Tweedle-Dee, suggest the image of progressive penology.

Just beyond the Education building the "walking" road intersects at a right angle the main road leading into camp from the prison gate and Rt. 15. We were prohibited from walking in that direction. By turning left, though, past New Industries (a long, white, windowless prefab structure, where office furniture for Washington executives is produced by prisoners at the rate of 7¢, 12¢, up to 45¢ per hour), and then beyond the steam pipe that trestle-like goes over the road behind the little shack and lone pump on the left that serves as a gas station, and the sloping, well-tended lawn of the Mechanics Division building on the right, one finally enters upon a long flat stretch of road, fields on each side. When I first entered this jail, this road ended for us at the old sandstone church, used for Sunday services, that hides somewhat guiltily behind huge old trees: it is the sole survivor of the village it once served, all the houses of which were razed when this area was appropriated by the Federal government for use as a munitions plant before World War II. The old stone foundations, like forgotten monuments, are barely noticeable in the fields along the road. Across the road from the church is a small prisoner-tended cemetery with stones dating back to Revolutionary days. When I first arrived at the Allenwood prison, we were permitted to walk to the church, but our leash was tightened by paranoid administrators, faced with inmate-tapped phone lines from the church phone and increasing evidence of contraband. High on one of the telephone poles that stretch the whole length of that road, like so many crucifixions historically considered, they nailed a sign which read: "No pedestrian traffic beyond this point except for church services on Sunday morning."

The second sign of Spring: The joggers, the weight-lifters, and the ballplayers—accomplishment bound. The joggers came in all sizes, all ages. A retired Lieutenant Colonel (a Southern military man) in his late fifties, distinguished gray-black hair and slight pouch, in on a six-month bit for tax evasion, really began jogging, one of a few, in January, and kept it up through Spring. As often as he jogged to the cemetery and back, he would boast of it each time he returned; he was impressed by his increasing endurance in the company of younger men who did not jog and older men who could not. When Spring arrived, his time of release, the colonel had lost more weight than he had anticipated; the pouch was gone but so too were the fleshy cheeks and leisured double chin. He was thin and pale, eyes newly sunken and tearful. He shaved his sideburns when another prisoner pointed out that they were simply gray, no longer distinguished, just old. The unselected company of convicts was not much to his liking, but what really got to him was his job assignment: he was an assistant orderly and helped a friendly but hapless Black, also from Maryland, clean the shithouse.

The Black Muslims would jog also, singly or in groups. As

groups they moved in the military manner, three abreast, in unison, heels striking the road in time, and they would give ground to nobody. Especially after the riot of January 1970 in the Lewisburg prison, which involved their brothers now in segregation, and one result of which for the Muslims at Allenwood was the elimination of all hitherto approved and scheduled periods of exercise (marching and karate), study, and worship, they were on the road jogging in earnest, faces taut but without expression, eyes unfocused, fists clenched. Unlike the colonel who jogged in khaki, the Muslims wore sweat shirts (some with the crescent-and-star symbol magic-markered on the back) and sweat pants over which they would wear a pair of cut-off khakis the length of Bermuda shorts. They ran in boots rather than sneakers and spoke to no one, nor acknowledged any nod. Even those who were students of mine would not exchange greetings when I encountered them on the road.

It was always sad to see the clenched faces go by in an otherwise almost pastoral setting of field, wood, cows, and ever lively cloud-bescattered sky. The intensity of their contempt for the "white devils" demanded a ritual to contain it, and, having lost their foot-stomping, rage-inspiring sessions, they chose to jog. And jog they did: by as many as eighty or ninety Hereford cows with as many calves, black with white markings, tawny-colored, or fair-haired, and regular Hereford red and white calves, all bright in the sun, frolicking among the cows and each other, licking and being licked, butting and being butted out of the way. When hungry they would ram their foreheads into their most contented mother's udder and play with her teats as puppies do with a bone.

Nor were the calves the only ones to play near that pasture road. In Spring some prisoners, responding to other needs, would fashion a lasso and try to play John Wayne to one of the bulls, if there were any, or cows in the field. City men all, they soon gave up the rope and went for the tail.

Along this pasture road, too, the farthest point from the hack's eyes in the Administration building, an acid-head and a young C.O. from Richmond, Virginia, both tall lanky men, flew their huge kite, constructed out of a sheet, wire clothes hangers, nylon cord copped from Industries, and bearing on it the International Peace Symbol ☮, the C.O.'s mark, and a silhouette of a rhinoceros, the mark of the acid head. They made, too, out of the cardboard tube from a roll of toilet paper, a capsule for a diapered and parachute-burdened frog, a pet from the courtyard off the dormitory corridor where these two made their hectic home. When the kite was already high in the sky, the capsulated frog with chute was sent up the kite's string by an affixed sail. Upon reaching the knotted joint of the kite's lines, with the speed provided by the capsule's sail, the frog was jolted backward out of his haven, smashing the paper barrier, and came floating downward—weird sight!—and landed not so gently in the Education building's parking lot, his thighs a little scraped by cinders and, after that, the only frog in camp with a blown mind.

Beyond this pasture was a wood thick with pine, birch, maple, and oak. As in many woods, the lowest limb line seemed uniform across the breadth of the woods, providing a black margin of tree trunk above which the newly budding trees became an ever-enriched green mass as Spring turned to summer; in the fall the same black border line framed the chaotic, myriad-colored autumn leaves. This wood was, besides a delight to see every day, a repository of many a "stash" of contraband, carried there from the cyclone fence that surrounds the entire plantation, especially where Rt. 15 skirts along the camp's eastern edge. Along that route, and it is not news to any administrator, on the other side of Penny Hill, the "drops" are made—whiskey, dope, "groceries," i.e., roasts, clams, Italian and Puerto Rican specialties of all sorts—and then transported to this farther wood where they are buried in large cans or plastic bags or whatever. "Hootch," homemade brew, is also brewed and stashed in this wood. So it is not unusual to see among the grazing cattle some awkward yet swift-moving brown shapes, almost on all fours, trotting from road to wood or from wood to road, arms laden with goodies. To see but not to see is the game, especially if the runners have a man on point, that is a friend standing on the road as nonchalantly as a cop on stakeout.

Beyond that wood is more field and then the mountain that runs parallel to the camp, the long and unpeaked wall of this prison valley. In northeastern Pennsylvania, the small town of Palmerton, where I grew up, was located in a valley quite similar to this one; it had an identical mountain bordering it, scarred by a similar fire-break from top to bottom, and dipped into a gap at exactly the same spot half a mile north; at night the towers on the mountains, both that of my youth and of my imprisonment, gave forth the same red glow. Two towers when I was young; six at the end of three decades. Beyond the gap near the prison, on the other side of the mountain, was Williamsport; but since I had never seen it I had to accept it on faith. I knew the road winding through the gap was Rt. 15 and that it skirted the outer boundaries of the campgrounds; that Penny Hill looked down upon Rt. 15 and, standing on the hill, one could see the valleys and river of this central Pennsylvania area stretch out for miles and miles. Yet to one confined as I was to the compound, New York City or Paris were as near as Williamsport, hell, a hell of a lot closer, and that lethargic mountain, for all I knew or cared, had but one side and it never moved.

But if it never moved, some of us did. David Geary, poet and fellow resister, was released to our great delight one fair, fine day in May 1969. Never were the old paradoxes about parting so futile: such unselfish pleasure and rich joy at his release demanded I walk. So down to the church I went (for at that time we were still allowed to make that walk) and sat upon the steps. Across the road the small cemetery stood shaded by a huge pine tree, which from where I sat seemed cut from some Japanese silk screen; the black spear-pointed gate was open as if for customers. Before me about ten miles away a mountain range ran into our fellow-traveler of this valley at a right angle, but a haze tauntingly obscured the intersecting lines. (That notch where the two mountains merged was called "Nagasaki Notch" by my good friend Tom, who was there at Hiroshima and Nagasaki in one of the tracing planes attached to the bombing mission). My ears delighted in the songs of the birds, my eyes danced to their feeding and flight: red-winged blackbirds, robins, sparrows, crows in the distance over the pastures; the sun bathed my face and all the green grass in front of me, the rich

Spring / 17

texture of the fields rolling away toward the mountain with only the barest hint of the farm buildings hidden to their tops by trees—all of this green and golden morning made me completely forget about time, and, so delighted on so many levels, I missed the noontime count, left Time in a hack's hand, missed the calls for recount, delayed the chow lines and the work details, and was only brought back to jail by the official who intruded into my vision in a truck, all kinds of angry threats upon his lip, harassment in his eyes. But I could only laugh and smile, for even on the trip back to the Administration building by truck (to have my wrists slapped) I was all green and birdsong, sun and an open gate—David Geary on his bus trip home.

At about the same time early in Spring, when sleepwalking to breakfast at six-thirty as the early morning mist hung heavy on the trees and fields beyond the compound, like bedrolls in a crash pad, and our own Americanized "rosy-fingered dawn" approached over the top of Penny Hill; when in the afternoons the uncontained roof of this valley was alive with sun-streaked, wind-blown clouds; then the lawn furniture for visitors and inmates on weekends would be brought out of storage and placed, newly painted, picnic-like, in the garden and walk outside the Administration building. And behind the Education building, the weight lifters would bring out the benches and weights from the dingy, damp hole that was their gym, and do their thing, stripped to the waist, for all who wished to see. Both actions were designed to impress: the visitors could sit and admire the beauty of the valley and rest assured that it was real and no great threat to their man, and the weight lifters proclaimed with grunts that they had a "thing" to keep their heads and bodies together. One short but hugely muscular inmate so lived his thing that, shortly after his release, he stole a car, was rearrested, and no doubt right back into it in the next joint he hit. He was so muscle-bound that to brush his teeth he would first have to crook his neck, as if to inspect his armpit.

Others, delighted with their bodies and other bodies, the "pitchers" and "catchers" who enjoyed "swapping"—the homosexuals, that is, would in Spring emerge from the darkened shit-houses and mop-closets of the dormitories to make the faggy-morning-in-the-field scene, or, in the evening under the mute stars they would meet in the dugouts on the softball field, where the next day my friend Tom, bank robber, Athletic Director, and foremost player, would find the rolls of soiled toilet paper and the discarded jockey shorts—not quite the silk handkerchiefs of more self-possessed days.

My hard-core friends who had done time in Lewisburg or other jails, state and federal, and were at Allenwood because they were "short-timers," would criticize and castigate me for walking alone on the roads as I frequently did. They carried over the patterns of behavior harder joints inflicted upon them, especially with regard to "homos" or "fags"—there one did not walk alone but always with a partner, so that the image of a loner (one unprotected and, hence, easily, "ripped off"—raped) would not be projected. Since no one I knew of ever came to Allenwood directly, especially the resister types, we all have had the experience of a county jail or a Lewisburg A and O (administration-and-orientation) unit, where one is oriented not only to the prison programs but to prisoner life styles as well. Some fare better than others. None come through unscarred, psychically or physically. It remains, even in prison, the least-talked-about segment of our experience.

On that pasture road, then, by the placid, guileless cows, tails busy with flies, the homosexuals would "swish" their way, with perhaps half the energy they would put into it in the corridors of Lewisburg; they retained still the tight-fitting pants and the blue handkerchief with its flying phallic tip, beckoning from the back pocket on the right side.

Down that road, also, at speeds adjusted to their resentment toward idling prisoners, the hacks would drive their detail trucks with one or two inmates aboard; or, administrators alone or with visitors, would cruise in black station wagons and observe the workings of their feudal estate. It is feudal in the sense that, though guidelines for prison procedures exist in liberal measure and character, as the various heads of the Bureau of Prison keep in step with at least the rhetoric of modern penology, each prison is run by its warden or whatever power base obtains, regardless of guidelines. The hacks, last on the ladder of power in relation to administrators, but first in relation to prisoners, face an eight-hour shift, slightly more than the minimum wage, six days a week, work assignments, and men not eager to work. Unlike the prisoners, their "time" (and they refer to it as "time"—"I got eight more years to go on this bit," i.e., before retirement) is not the State's but their own responsibility. A prisoner evades work, generally, as he evades time; the hack must supervise the evasion and frequently do what has not been done. In Spring, when more and more the idle prisoners are visible on the roads at all times during the day, the hacks become short-tempered, demand more of their own details, and busy themselves with the hustles of the idlers.

The most humane of the hacks I found to be the alcoholics. They have tasted misery. They seldom worked men very hard, let slip by more than the game calls for, and were easily conned into quitting work to hang around a shack and play cards or climb in the trucks and drive away the rest of the morning or afternoon on the remote side roads and unused parts of this 4,000-acre or more plantation.

Down that road—down that road five, ten, fifteen times a day walk the broken, the torn-up, lonely and fucked up men, alone or with partners. Either their bodies sag, shoulders bow, arms fall as if with weights bound; or they charge the shadow-infested daylight, chest heaving, arms swinging, and who can tell if they are running toward or away from the creatures of their minds? Hard Time.

Hard Time, as opposed to Good Time, can result from hassles in the jail, homosexual assault, threats, debts, harassment from hacks and administrators; but usually the time referred to is that during which all of a man's energies, his thoughts, his dreams, his fantasies, all his fettered sorrow, impotent rage, and helpless fears are "on the street," where whatever is disintegrating, dead, or dying—his love, his principles, his family, case or dreams— is disintegrating, dead, or dying beyond his ability to share, help, or prevent it. Good Time is time spent inside the jail— active, thoughtless, distracted, swift. But Hard Time never moves: it is mind-consuming, bitter, concentrated, and stagnant.

Bowels twist and knot. Hours turn into yesterdays, days become fantasized tomorrows, and tomorrow awaits incredible exposures. Hard Time stays lumped up in the chest to spoil meals, yearn for violence, make days dark and nights bright with anxiety endlessly tossing, marked by the face-seeking flashlight of the hack as he makes his "count." The cup of Spring is drained and broken.

And on the road in such anguish, every stone shouts of impotence, every cow blissfully insults, each calf is a heavy burden. How can blossoms soften limbs long naked? Why do swallows dart away? Why do white birds hover over the wood? These blue and golden flowers by the roadside betray. This gentle breeze is trapped outside dormitory doors. Everything bothers, hates, and is hated. The sight of men beginning again—pleased! —fighting for straws. All this Spring-bedeviled valley becomes a hell to him who winters in his head.

The Walk

RECORD OF GOOD TIME FORFEITURE

U. S. PENITENTIARY, LEWISBURG, PA.

Name: COOK, John A. *No.* 35406-134 *Date hearing* 5/12/70
Good time allowance ....
Good time earned to date of violation: ....
Statement of Violation: OUT OF BOUNDS—DISOBEYING A
DIRECT ORDER.

At approximately 2:50 P.M., on May 3, 1970, while confined at
the Allenwood Prison Camp, Cook together with four other
inmates entered the field just east of the administration building
and began walking toward the front entrance. Mr. H. L. Mc-
Kinnis, Food Administrator, approached them and ordered them,
individually, to stop and return to the compound. They ignored
the order and kept walking.

Mr. Rauch, Associate Warden (O), informed Cook that this
was a Good Time Forfeiture Board Hearing. Further, this committee designated by the Warden is meeting for the purpose of
determining whether or not they should recommend to the
Warden that all or part of his good time be forfeited for the
offenses described above. Cook admitted that the charges were
true. Cook said his object in doing this was for the group of
demonstrators at the front entrance to see him and vice versa.
Cook also admitted attending a meeting with a group of inmates
a few days prior to the demonstration in which they discussed
the upcoming demonstration. Cook was notified at the conclu-
sion of the hearing of the committee's recommendation to the
Warden and that he would be advised of the final decision. He
was also advised that if the Warden concurs with the Good

Time Forfeiture Board's recommendation, he could appeal the decision to the Director through the Prisoners' Mail Box.

Officer reporting violation: H. L. McKinnis, Food Administrator

Penalty recommended by Good Time Forfeiture Board:

(1) 20 DAYS S.G.T.   W. H. RAUCH, Assoc. Wdn. (O), Chairman

(2) 20 DAYS S.G.T.   R. L. HENDRICKS, Assoc. Wdn. (P)

(3) 20 DAYS S.G.T.   O. DAINOFF, Chief, Class.-Parole

I hereby impose the following penalty on the above-named prisoner: Forfeiture of 20 DAYS S.G.T.

OR   AW(P)
Original to Record Office   J. J. PARKER, WARDEN
co-Bureau   *Date* May 12, 1970

Such is the form of justice in a prison; firmly established rules of conduct were openly violated: five prisoners left the compound in broad daylight, in sight of the prison population and some of the over forty additional hacks, as well as the administrators of Allenwood and Lewisburg, who were patrolling the road, and walked toward the front gate of the prison, and they continued to walk after being ordered to halt. Penal severity, as clearly defined as lightning, demanded that those obstructionists of stable laws, rooted like the lethargic mountain nearby, be penalized and disciplined in order to intimidate the heedless and make other men avoid transgressions. Force must be used. Let the jaws of justice bite upon them.

The form of justice. The form of human life in prison results, indeed, from clearly defined and firmly established rules of conduct, the most defined and firmly established rule being Thou Shalt Not Escape or Try To Escape. But the rules of conduct of an institution that should not exist; the penal arm of a Federal government that long ago lost, if it ever had, the consent of the governed and should itself no longer exist; those rules of conduct do but conduct an abomination. And when so perverse a dark principle as penal justice encounters its opposite, love, then form has combined with content and a new, unprecedented act occurs. The eyes of Camus' judge-penitent are not needed to distinguish guilt or innocence here.

I was being provided for that Friday evening, the first of May, by Mexico, a tall perfectly proportioned narcotics smuggler and the new headman of the clothing room, who was paying me in terms of four new khaki pants and an equal number of light-weight khaki shirts, also new, new jockey shorts and T-shirts, and, as a bonus, a pair of custom-made white tennis shorts (a snip or two of scissors and kitchen whites were so trans-formed), in the back room of "The Jungle" that served as cloth-ing issue, supplies store, laundry drop and pickup, and hangout, at this time, for the Puerto Rican element in camp.

Mexico was a student of mine; the new outfit was his way of paying me back for the teaching I was into in the school that functioned, for me and the other inmates involved, as a hustle with bouts of "good time"—that is, time "out" of our personal problems, the hang-up of jail, and time filled with nouns, pro-nouns, verbs, and comments on Western Civilization.

Mexico, for all his tightly knit muscular body (he represented the "heavy punch" Puerto Ricans could call upon in rumbles if they had to), was extremely shy with gringos and very sensitive, especially about his limited ability in English. He seldom spoke; he preferred to move slowly, intense and self-contained, through groups of inmates, as if his silences and his presence were suf-ficient. An admirable man, Mexico.

"Do you know that guy? The tall one on the left?" he asked as he handed me the white shorts, while pointing out the open window toward my two delightful friends, David Rumon and Jerry Foster, who were already lounging in the field between the new dorms, awaiting the meeting soon to take place, the one referred to by the Good Time Forfeiture Board in its report to Warden Parker.

"Yes, I know him," I answered.

"Give him this, then," and he handed me a can of tooth

powder. "He asked for it earlier."

"He got it already," came the reply from the Puerto Rican at the sewing machine, who had just double-stitched the white shorts.

"Okay," said Mexico.

And I understood, as I handed back the can of powder, his eyes locked on mine, that he was telling me that he would provide for David and Jerry, too, as friends of mine. I nodded thanks and left with my "score" held fast in my arms, a crazy glee stirring within me.

"What you so happy for, Hobbit?" David asked as he came off his back to a sitting position on the green grass as I approached.

"Turn that smile off. What you got? Gifts for us?" asked Jerry, rocking back and forth in a homemade lawn chair, the upper section of a dismantled iron-rung chair.

"No, gifts for me," I said. "I just scored off Mex. New pants, shirts, underwear, everything. Even white tennis shorts."

"Put 'em on, Hobbit! You gotta wear them for the meeting. It'll be great," David cried.

"The Hobbit in white shorts," Jerry mused. "Put them on or sit down now and turn that crazy smile off."

The corners of my mouth were, indeed, aching, and I turned away to return with my goodies to my home in Number 4 dorm, "the honor dorm" as the administrators referred to it; for unlike the other dorms, this one had cubicles that provided a little privacy. I had submitted a "copout" (prisoner request form) to get in, and, remembering Kierkegaard, I joked at the time that any special favor was an embarrassment. So I colored myself embarrassed, yet delighted in the small cube, where I could read and smoke and think and not have to observe all that was going down around me. I had good neighbors, too: Blacks, fore and aft; a quiet Polish workingman and a writer, rewriting his novel in the evenings for the fifth time, on larboard; and, most comforting of all, a white-washed cement block wall on the starboard side. Nat, the Black whose corner cube was in front of mine, a shared window on the courtyard between us, shipped (and smuggled dope) as a cook in the merchant marine before he was busted. He cooked in the mess hall, and he provided

Johnny, the Black at my back, and me with eggs and other extras from the kitchen.

"Have some chicken, Jack," a dark voice would say, and over the partition separating us the oval eggs would arch.

In my cube, then, I quickly stashed my new clothes in my locker, made a bundle out of the old ones to be taken care of later, and changed into white tennis shorts and T-shirt. Then I retraced my steps and found about 25 C.O.'s and a few other inmates, most of them sitting like so many spring-clad Buddhas cross-legged in a circle in the middle of the meadow between the dorms.

"I told them to wait for you, Hobbit," David said. "Sit here, Hobbit."

And I settled down between David and Jerry. The sun had yet to set beyond the mountain in front of us, and I watched that orange ball spread a thousand shades of blue and a thousand colors of red into the sky, while the rapping went on, nervous and loud as it always was at the beginning of one of these meetings. Everyone dumped on meetings. They were futile, absurd ego-trips. Bad for the head. All the criticism and jokes could not hide, however, our anxiety about them; for as futile as they appeared, out of them usually came something we knew would change the routine, our current comfortable rut, and that possibility was looked upon with dread.

I was not eager for what was to come and decided I would wait and bide my time. The sunset was extraordinary, if the rapping was not, and David, Jerry, and I just sat and watched it.

Bob Eaton, Quaker Action Group organizer from Philadelphia and Captain of the peace ship *Phoenix*, began in his earnest manner to outline why we were all gathered together.

"There's going to be a demonstration on Sunday," he announced to the already aware and anxious group.

It is time to go inside the heads, to penetrate gently the minds of the political prisoners, as the spring breezes, following one upon the other, stir their psyches; for only then can that term "demonstration," as well as the reality of that antiprison demonstration of May 3, 1970, to which we responded, be understood.

The Walk / 29

In ancient China it was thought meritorious if during the hunt three kinds of game were caught: those that served as offerings to the gods, those for feasting guests, and those for everyday consumption. When the catch answered all three purposes, the hunt was considered especially successful. So it goes with demonstrations and those free enough to participate in or organize them. A demonstration should serve primarily as a meaningful offering to our personal gods, whether they be household idols, such as ideologies and simple life styles; or, better, principles; or best (in my opinion) principle and conscience together and entire under the banner most authentically and recently proclaimed by Che Guevera: "Let me say, with the risk of appearing ridiculous, that the true revolutionary is guided by great feelings of love." Second, a demonstration should provide for the feasting guests; that is, the demonstrators in solidarity and sympathy with each other and with all men and women in danger and oppressed, voluntarily place themselves, by their act, in danger and so dissolve the distinctions of time and place, class and ideology, of race and nationality, and attempt thereby, again with Che, to "graduate as human beings." Third, demonstrations should provide sustenance for those for whom the demonstration was made, for those not participating, those too weak or hung up at the time who were not guests at the feast, and for the many others who, through no real fault of their own, have not this means at their disposal of feeding their psyches. But by observing a demonstration that does not alienate, and by coming into contact with those who participated, this audience vicariously participates in the statements being made and, more or less, identifies with those making them. When a demonstration answers all three purposes, it may, I think, be said to be especially successful.

Just prior to my entering jail in January 1969, a "Celebration of Conscience" demonstration, organized by peace and resistance groups, was held at Allenwood. According to the main organizer, the demonstration at the prison would have qualified under all three heads; but it one were to believe the response of the prisoners, political and otherwise, it would appear to have failed on every level. The threefold catch were chimera.

In Allenwood at that time, working as a clerk and teacher in the Education department, was a free-lance writer and "bad-check artist," a regular con in his late twenties, who "jailed with"—i.e., spent his time hanging around—the political prisoners. He wrote an article about the "Celebration of Conscience" event. Nonpolitical prisoner that he was, he approached the thing, not only with his own peculiarly obnoxious cynicism, but with the acculturated cynicism of the regular con, viewing the antics of political types whose views and life styles were hardly comprehensible. His tone in that essay, which mirrored the way hard-core inmates viewed the activities of the Peace Movement, inside and outside of prison, was bitter; his judgments were oblique and his humor somewhat addled. He made clear, however, that the "Celebration of Conscience" failed because it isolated political prisoners from the rest of the population, and thereby nourished neither the C.O.'s nor the other inmates.

The C.O.'s in prison at that time, as he delightedly reported, were livid about the demonstration for a number of reasons, the foremost of which was that they were not consulted about it, and hence they felt they were being "used" by the Peace Movement; for the latter, in order to have any demonstration at all, had to make significant concessions to the administration of the prison. The C.O.'s felt hoodwinked and called it a "Symbolic farce."

The principal organizer of the event thought differently, however. He admitted that the C.O.'s were being "used," but he maintained that it was done to arouse people on the street to the issues of amnesty and resistance. He felt the event was organized primarily for the white middle-class types who wished to find some way of celebrating the consciences of resisters in prison, rather than for the resisters themselves. He concluded that the resisters in prison, the visitors, the "hacks," and the local townspeople were all being used in "one grand holy conspiracy."

The "holy conspiracy" did not fill the pit of the hard core's rancor with "love" and "peace" and the desire for the "beloved community" as the organizer of the street suggested that it should. The "holy conspiracy" left the community of resisters torn and shattered; it created a wedge between the resisters and the other inmates, thereby destroying any possibility for "beloved community" within the camp; and, finally, it left intact, crystallized in fact, the mistrust, sarcasm, and prejudice non-political inmates traditionally direct toward political prisoners. Underneath the hard-core criminal's bitterness there is a lonely man paying unaccustomed attention to, perhaps, a viable alternative—community, peace, however he framed it—the demonstration of which but threw him deeper into bitterness. There is merit to his cynicism, I think, for it tries to cover a painful desolation; there is little merit, on the other hand, to "one grand holy conspiracy" that was neither grand nor holy but did conspire with the conditions already existing in Allenwood prison to create havoc in the heads of prisoners.

"There's going to be a demonstration on Sunday," Bob Eaton announced to the already aware and anxious group. He liked structure.

But this time it would be an antiprison demonstration, not a Celebration of Conscience; for the C.O.'s had been consulted and the consensus of those at all interested in another demonstration was that it be directed against the prison system and for all prisoners, not just political types. David Dellinger, architect of the Peace Movement and one of the defendants in the recent Chicago 8 trial, would be the main speaker. An anticipated crowd of over a thousand was expected to congregate at the Allenwood camp gate beside the public golf course. It was organized by Philadelphia Resist and the local Bucknell people, among them the historian Richard Drinnon.

"We have to decide if we are going to respond to the demonstration," Eaton concluded, "and if so, in what way?"

Rather than answer to so direct a challenge, the group responded with all the latest rumors:

"I heard the owner of the golf course was closing down Sunday," Alex Futterman offered.

"Three thousand longhairs sitting on the fence. They'll go mad!" shouted Bill Boss, who looked more like a biker than a resister.

The Walk / 32

"What if they lock us in during the thing?" worried Billy "The Librarian" outloud.

"Work Release guys say the whole town's talking about it," Mike, a Black militant and veteran of the civil rights marches, put in. The Work Release program allows certain trusted prisoners to work in factories and other low-key employment outside the prison during the day. The prisoners return to their quarters at night.

"Engle's gonna shit bricks," Eaton said, catching the trend. "They were in plotting all morning." R. R. Engle, Supervisor of the Allenwood Prison Camp, is a small man whose nickname is "Railroad."

"More fucking overtime for the hacks," sneered the bored Dan Kelly.

"Are they planning any action other than rapping?" Beach "the Marxist" asked.

"All those chicks. Those legs. Those cunts. All that hair!" Jerry, beside himself, was rolling in the grass.

"Never get a thousand here," Tony, artist and beautiful Black from Providence, Rhode Island, out of Cape Verde Island, remarked. "There's a march in Washington on Sunday. Chavez, I think. And something is going down in Boston with the Panthers."

And so the empty bowl of our meeting was filled by anxieties, rumors, quips, and gripes. It must have appeared, as indeed it was, chaotic and unstructured to Slim, Tom, and one or two other nonpolitical prisoners who were lounging or standing nearby. Any unscheduled meeting is a matter of curiosity to prisoners, as it is a thing prohibited by the authorities. But meetings generally have order and no order was evident here; leaders and no leaders came forth here; agenda and no agenda was followed here. Just the ravings of the eccentric, undisciplined, hung up, ego-tripping, and playful C.O.'s. Tom, who left at this point, told me afterward that he was surprised we ever got anything accomplished, when so few seemed willing to get down to business.

He wondered how we ever got together on the Chandler issue, when each C.O. seemed to go in his own direction. Richard

The Walk / 33

Chandler is a young C.O. at the Lewisburg prison who refuses to cooperate with prison authorities in any way; he refuses to work, eat, walk, or do anything on command. They locked him up in the Lewisburg "hole," the segregation unit, for close to nine months. When he became too much of a hassle for them to cope with, they tried to transfer him to the Springfield Penitentiary in Springfield, Illinois, a combination prison and asylum for the criminally insane. When the C.O.'s at Allenwood heard of it, they organized and prevented that transfer. Chandler is still in the "hole" at Lewisburg. He prefers that to Springfield. But Tom found our present meeting too confusing, for he was a born organizer.

Slim, who looked, talked, sang, and walked like a ridge runner, bootlegger, "Mountain William" as Tony called them, but was actually in jail on a tax evasion bit, and had been beaten close to death at Springfield Federal Penitentiary, where he was sent for threatening a hack who was hassling him, said little but absorbed much. He shared our contempt for government, prisons, and laws. A farmer and dairyman, son of a farmer and dairyman, he had the independence and reserve of men used to doing with their hands. He, too, thought the meeting strange.

"Somebody suggested this afternoon that we smuggle a message out to them," said Eaton, trying again. "That surely we can do. Tomorrow's Saturday and some of us have visits coming."

"Yeah."

"Right on!"

"Write it up."

"Kite it out."

"Sell 'em a ticket!"

"Sell it. Sell it!" came the voices from the ring: the message was unanimously cheered.

"Let's make it heavy, so heavy it'll take a committee of them to read it," shouted the now eager Dan.

"Who's going to write it?" asked Alex.

"All of us," came the fierce reply.

"Wait a minute. Wait! How can all of us write one message?" Eaton, sensing chaos, put in. "Let's settle on one or two, let them write it, and pass it around for approval later."

"But one or two can't cover it all," Beach objected. "Let's have six or seven, each writing his own, and then put it all together. In the reading room."

"Yeah, who can speak for all of us, anyway?"

"Yeah, let's do that," was the group's reply, and they began offering each other, choosing, and those into the message began thinking of a clique.

"Get the Chicago people in," cried Boss. And it looked as if the meeting would be the message.

"And the Weathermen," Dan insisted. "Angry Arabs, too," he added.

"And the Panthers in Detroit," said Beach.

"Don't knock the Cong," Back the punster quipped.

David was shaking his head nervously. He settled down to cracking his joints by stretching out each arm, each leg, finally twisting his neck. He cracked all over. He resembled one of El Greco's serene young nobles in a sudden fit of anxiety. He sensed the thunder and lighting as the sun declined and tensions rose.

"Okay. Okay." Eaton interjected quickly as he tried to steer some direction into the gathering. "We've got the message settled. Kelly, Beach, Colmar, Futterman, and whoever else will do it in the reading room of 3 and 4 after the meeting. Then get it to us all by 'lights out.' Okay? We can get it out tomorrow afternoon."

Across from me, Dickey "the Worm" Wiley, squatting on his heels, was keening to his own rhythm, rocking back and forth and whistling the blues through the gaps between his teeth. Speed freak, it was all a trip to him.

"There are other things we might do," again Eaton began. "I was thinking about painting "Right On" on the roof of the Administration building. Now . . ." and he was drowned out in a chorus of suggestions.

"On the road do it in big white letters," someone threw in.

"Should have a balloon with 'Right On' on it."

"A kite!" Billy shouted. "Where's Junior's kite?"

"Let's run our own flag—a red one—up the flagpole," Dan offered, laughing now loud and bitterly.

The Walk / 35

"We can wear red arm bands all day long," said Colmar "the Trotskyite."

"You're just playing kid's games," objected George, an organizer for the McCarthy campaign.

"It's a Sunday, so we can't quit work," puzzled Billy "the librarian."

"Paint 'Right On' in the hallway and the mess hall," Bill Boss suggested. "It's better there. And we can paint the 'Snake' there, too"—his large frame in dirty kitchen whites doubled over in laughter.

"Yeah, Engle 'the snake,'" and, palms cupped, elbows grasped, the self-proclaimed signature and self-image of our camp superintendent was striking all around.

"He is a fucking redneck snake," Boss said, irritation rising in him. "Did you hear what he said to me about the can of peaches? The dirty, pint-sized, mother fucking little monster . . ."

At that point, glee-gone and anxious that my thoughts not scatter under the barrage of words now filling the ring, I asked Bill Boss if I might make a suggestion.

"Sure, Hobbit, go to it, my man," and he settled down to listen and suddenly there was a stillness all around.

"I agree with the first suggestion already made," I began and sought out the eyes of those looking at me. "The message to the demonstrators. But I would argue that that is the least we could do; it is expected by them, I should think. And if we didn't give them one, I'm sure the organizers would make one up of their own. It's obvious. That must be done.

"And I agree, too, with the prank business. I'd prefer a black flag—"

"You would!" Dan shouted at me, eyes flashing.

"Yes, I would," I replied quickly, not wanting to lose the floor, "a large black flag, a painted sheet, flying from the top of that chimney near the powerhouse, where it would be visible to the people at the gate and the hacks couldn't get it down in a hurry, either. Who can see the flagpole but us? What good, then?

"The pranks are good but not enough. The message is a must. What I want to suggest, and I think we are capable of it after the Chandler business, and I think it is the most obvious response and the most political response to an antiprison demonstration we could make, is that we walk, as many as we can muster, down the road and to the gate and try to meet the demonstrators. We will be walking to a guaranteed bust. I doubt if we'd ever get there, but if we can get within sight of them—" and I was cut off sharply.

"No. No. You're way off base," Beach cried, his arm in a gesture of repulsion. The bowl began to crack audibly.

"Hey, man," said Boss, fatherly and concerned, "that's Escape! To walk down that road. Do you know how many hacks are gonna be here on Sunday? I heard from McKinnis about fifty plus all the regulars and Hendricks, Rauch, the works. You'll never make it. Or you'll make a two-year bit for escape."

"It isn't Escape—or they can't call it that anyway—if we do it in broad daylight with Rauch and them watching," I countered.

Heads were shaking, bodies squirming, everyone was into as well as out of themselves. Into their own scene, hurried and hassled: how much time in front, Parole Board coming up, busts or no busts, good chance or none; some, like Kelly, were short enough to see the end in a month's time; others worried about parents, wives, and their job assignments; all saw the violence, the guaranteed bust to the "hole." And they were looking out of themselves: at the group. How are they taking it? Not good. Everyone's uptight. See what happens.

"Crazy, man, no good. No good," came the gut response.

"You wouldn't get an inch into the road."

"It would be all over."

"No one would see it even but us."

"What good, then?"

"Like the flagpole. You said yourself." The voices, sharp and excited, seemed to be coming out of everyone.

"Can't hack this scene," yelled Tony. "Wow! The tensions here. All bad!" And all of us gathered had never been so apart, so brittle.

"What's political about it?" Dan demanded.

"It's an antiprison demonstration, right?" I shouted. "The first I've heard about anyway, right? Peace people at a prison gate, right? Hacks and administrators, walkie-talkies and trucks all

The Walk / 37

over, right? No prisoners—wrong! We have to complete the equation. Give the people what they came for. They came for prisoners. So we don't get down to them, so they see us being busted. It's better than not seeing any prisoners at all, right?"

"Wrong!" Dan boomed.

"It's the only generous thing to do," I said, straining with the tension in my own head. "How many times, Dan," a hardness in my voice I did not like, but "fuck it," "have we picketed at Washington or at the U.N. and never saw the bloody people we were there for?"

John Hogan, the gentle ex-Maryknoll brother who, with the Berrigans and others, lit the Catonsville fire, moved into the burning space between Dan and me and questioned whether or not we might not be upsetting the demonstration, messing with it, and he wondered if we had a right to do that.

"I don't know if we have the right, John," I said, aware that I was still bristling, yet thankful to him for the gentle question. "I've heard the rumor that at least some of the Bucknell people are thinking of a walk *into* the camp. If civil disobedience is a part of the demonstration, I don't see how a walk *out* of the camp by us could upset anything. Add to the fun, I should think.

"It would be good in here, too. How many guys dream of walking out of this joint? How many? How often?"

But nothing helped. Some carried their fidgeting away to their homes, disgruntled, confused, and annoyed.

"Don't worry, Hobbit," Jerry said quietly as I let myself sink back on the grass, stretched out my shaking legs, and looked at the spreading dusky sky, an uneven graying darkness. All the colors were gone. I lifted my head briefly. The mountain was black.

"Yeah, Hobs, those'll go who'll go," David piped in. "Meetings are shit, Hobbit, you know that."

"Yeah, shit," I said.

"Don't let it get ya, Hobbit," he said. "See that star?"

"What star? Where?" I asked.

"Damn, you need glasses, Hobbit. Here, take mine," and I put David's glasses on and saw the star he was pointing to.

"Neat," I said. "Somewhat famished, I think. Kinda weak."

The Walk / 38

Eaton tried to put it together. "There's clearly not a consensus on any kind of walk. Let's go ahead with the message, anyway."

With that, the idea of a walk out of bounds to a bust seemed safely beaten down, and those opposed now eagerly came together to get the message written.

"Come on. Over to the reading room," they called in unison. The gathering ended. It began to rain.

David and I stood under the roof of the back porch of Number 3 and 4 Dorm and watched the gentle rain streak through the yellow cones of light shed by the powerful lamps high above the road, the tall poles deep in the bank of Penny Hill. The fine glimmering lines would then disappear into the darkness below, finally to emerge, anonymous and lost, and fall into puddles on the road before us. Those powerful lamps, the same as found at entrances and exits of state thruways and parkways, were not there when I first arrived at Allenwood; then I watched night fall and stars climb over Penny Hill. But since the bright lights went up, designed unsuccessfully to foil inmates making "runs" for contraband over the hill, that view of the heavens was simply blacked out.

I was angry. My anger roared within and without me, as gusts of snow in a storm circle and so surround a tree, swaying drunkenly in the blast, that it blends with the storm-white mass behind it. And to be angry in prison is to be helplessly frustrated; for, having no outlet, the anger diffuses and whirls around every object, obscuring its lines. David was silent. And I paced the porch in a black mood and faced with each turn a different howling gust of my own discontent: I was angry with the C.O.'s for cheating themselves of an opportunity to do, in absolute freedom, a beautiful act; angry at the corrosive prison system that robs human life of its inborn capacity for beauty and turns even natural beauty, this soft night and gently falling rain, into a grotesque travesty of absurd effects; angry at the fall of an idea that I had ridden high on for weeks; angry at my anger, for I knew it meant a sleepless, anxious night.

And I was depressed. The casings of my psyche rattled; frost appeared on the windows of my soul. Bitterness bore to the

The Walk / 39

root of me: the wind Melville writes about in an early Civil War poem:

> I know a wind in purpose strong—
> It spins *against* the way it drives.
> What if the gulfs their slimed foundations bare?

There was nothing to affirm, I felt, and no one to affirm anything. As after a night of gale and gust the snow-covered hillside is left bare but for the branches torn from trees, so were my friends and the principles we shared left scattered on the bare ground of this prison experience.

So much was lost.

Within the political arena in which we lived—among the prisoners singly or in groups, together with the hacks and administrators here and at Lewisburg—there could be no finer occasion to prove that for those truly free this prison—with all its rules and regulations, threats and intimidations, fences and fear of the "hole"—despite all these phantoms and realities, we could still prove that this prison just did not exist in us, nor we within it. Given the slave-master, prisoner-jailer relationship that obtains, what finer, more poignantly rebellious and human act could there be than to walk, glad and free, out of the prison grounds and toward the gate, where crowds gathered in opposition to this and all other prisons?

Politics, in general, is a nightmare in which the Agnews and the Nixons appear with archetypal regularity. A man's "politics," however, for Plato or a prisoner, for a Trotsky or a Weatherman, for Quixote or a paperhanger, is a pipe dream into which more fantasy than reality is put. But, I, for one, would rather believe in pipe dreams than suffer the nightmare of an Agnew. Given the political realities of a prisoner's life such a walk would be his pipe dream come true. Plato lived to see his pipe dreams take form only to shatter under assassination and corruption. We who are concerned more with undermining than founding a state; more with the transforming of people into persons than with the reforming of institutions; more with values and principles than with laws and rules of conduct; more with love as

The Walk / 40

letting be than with love as making by force you into me—we should foster pipe dreams where we find them, make them come true if we can.

But my pipe dream, this first of May, had become a nightmare. A political martyrdom or simple suicide awaited him who walked alone or with only one other down that road. Actions of the "fucked up" are easily understood by prisoners, who have been tempted to them often enough, but they are even more easily dismissed. A single walker or two walkers would not make the point. The men who by night actually made escape attempts were the objects of much envy until they were caught. Then ridicule followed them everywhere. We could take the sting out of the ridicule by escaping into the "hole"—rude guests, not punished prisoners. But that could be done only by a group, rather than by one ego-tripping man, if it was to reach the minds of many men. It is one thing for a group, holding together and joyous, to perform a political act, a rite of sacrifice; it is quite another to make a bloody sacrifice out of oneself, to make an absurdity in the eyes of others.

It was about time for the nine o'clock count. David made a move to split. Then out of the doors in haste came the C.O.'s from their meeting, message in hand. They did not stop to show it to us. As each one passed by, I sought his eyes. After the first glance, there was no other. Instead each turned to his neighbor and began talking in loud, confident tones of the "meat" in the message. They did not speak at all to us.

"They've dummied up on us," said David with surprise.

"Yeah," I said. "The freeze is on. We're ostracized."

We looked at each other. Laughter stirred in our guts, and I nervously, he spontaneously, released it. Shrugging, David left, hopping, for his "home" in The Jungle. I turned for one last look at the rainy night. It was suddenly clear to me: only under such glaring lights must the rain end up as disturbing puddles on the road. Beyond, on the hill or in the fields under the stars, the rain falls on flowers, crops, on living things.

Back in my cube for count, I tried to piece together what was left of an idea, an action. My black mood had disappeared and some of the glee, for a yet unfathomed reason, had returned. Clearly, the C.O.'s were adamant. But there was David. And Jerry. And me. Two more and we might have a family, if not a movement. I realized, then, where the glee came from and where it was directed. My hard-core friends were going to be approached again, as they had been during the Chandler affair. And if the group walking consisted of C.O.'s and hard core, so much more powerful a statement could be made. The glee was aimed at the C.O.'s behind me, who obviously were not in need of such a good thing; and at the hard core in front, for the men I was to contact retained, though older than the C.O.'s, a capacity for play, a contempt for administrators, and a life style eccentric even for jail. I was delighted at the prospect.

"Coffee, Nat?" I asked over the partition.

"Not for me, Jack. I gotta cook eggs in the morning," and thinking of his four o'clock call, his head disappeared under the blanket. "Use my jug, if you want," came his voice, muffled and warmed.

"Thanks," and I picked up his jug, an Instant Milk jar with a carved wooden handle taped to it, and walked out into the corridor toward the shithouse for water.

"Hi, Mike," I said as I passed my safe-cracking, now "cat"-driving friend, stretched out on a top bunk, an old issue of *Playboy* in his hands.

"What ya into, Jack?" he asked.

"Gotta talk to ya, Mike. Catch ya in the morning, o.k.?"

"Later, then," he said and, sensing something was up, he chuckled.

In the busy shithouse, I found an empty sink and filled Nat's jug. There was no hot water because three or four guys, shrieking now under the hot taps, were already in the shower. A Black was giving his buddy a haircut with a razor blade, both men standing with backs arched over the sinks, heads close to the mirror. Some J.W.'s (Jehovah's Witnesses) were loudly discussing their softball game just over: "Shucks," "Gol darned," and "Golly" their epithets. The two doors to the shithouse, one opening to the corridor, the other to the TV room, opened and closed rhythmically, letting in and then shutting out the chatter from the corridor or the loud structured sounds from the TV room, as men from both directions, fingers fumbling with buttons or belts, steered their way to relief.

Friday evening in a jail. It is unimaginable, as Camus wrote. But this Friday evening I was going to pass up all the trips—the TV room trip, the back porch trip, the looking-at-the-stars trip, the Late Night Movie trip ("Change it! Change it!")—and settle down with a pipe, coffee, and a churning mind—my own trip. I could not do otherwise really, for whenever I saw or passed a C.O. it was clear that the freeze was still on.

Past Mike, oblivious to the noise around him, and back in my cube, I dug out my stinger, the gift of my hard-core Italian friend, from underneath the electric heating unit that ran along the base of the wall, unwrapped it, and plugged one end into the wall, the other into the jug. It took a while. It was a "street" stinger, made for soft-boiling eggs, not one of the inmate coils that boil water in ten seconds. But I had time. I prepared the coffee. From my Planters Peanut can with plastic top that served as a coffee jar, I lifted two spoonfuls of instant coffee into my rather stained cup; and, the water boiling, I poured it in and caught the aroma rising. It was really too hot to drink. So I filled one of my five pipes, suspended bowls up in a rack, like so many generous friends willing and able to help, set the coffee on the shelf attached to the locker, slipped out of my shoes, fixed the pillows (one more than regulation), and settled in for a long night's ruminating.

It was clear to me that all the energy that went into the message disguised a real indifference to the demonstration and a willingness to let an obvious response slip by as a radical one. The green algae and weeds of the tadpole-thriving ditch by the pasture road, into which we peered as often as we walked, could not hide the fact that the ditch held stagnant water. And it was inertia, prison-imposed inertia, that we all faced, lived in, remembered as yesterday, squatted on today, and looked unhappily to tomorrow. After the initial shock of the prison experience, a prisoner sees how structured it all is, how debilitating it can be to expose all of his energies all of the time to what is happening; how indifferent it is to him, after all. And gradually he economizes his gestures, limits his movements, tightens the circle of experiences until a round rut or ditch is formed that may, he hopes, provide a space for some of a prior self to show forth, perhaps even grow. But, since there are months to go, he should not hurry, should not rush into things. A ditch is at least a ditch, he thinks, a place. These faces nearby know me. That is my cup. Those are my letters. Those books tell this world I'm not to be taken too lightly. Let's not disturb this fucking universe. My ditch, green to me and hiding certain valuable things, is my ditch. That world I left and lost, the little hole I once occupied in it, is no more for me. Those out there cannot understand this here. If they are so eager to confront jails, let them become felons. There's room in The Jungle, empty lockers, sagging top-bunk "homes."

Algae and green weeds represent a certain life, but they also thrive amid decay. Decay consciously breeds guilt. And guilt moves in two directions: outwardly it justifies itself; hence the "freeze" on David and me and the "meat" in the message. Inwardly, it stirs—as the wind low across Penny Hill returns to us on the road, as a rainfall will enlarge that ditch—so guilt stirs remorse for principles once thriving in our heads. I was not about to give up on the C.O.'s; yet now was not the time to approach them. Time for stirring was needed. All day Saturday remained and Sunday morning.

Tomorrow I would contact Tom and Mike. Those two plus the three of us could do it, and, doing it, perhaps bring in some of the C.O.'s.

I poured the water remaining in Nat's jug into my cup and reheated it. The lights went out. It was ten o'clock. The murmuring of voices in raps in near and distant cubes (so must bees be conscious of their fellows in a comb) died down to whispers. Delightful dorm, this. More coffee, stash the stinger, another pipe, and we're off.

There are three ways of getting to the gate: by going straight down the road; by going over the fields in a direct line from the rear of the Administration building; or, by entering the woods running parallel to the road, to use the cover of the trees until we emerge within one hundred yards of the gate. The first would provide visibility but make it quite easy for the hacks to stop us; the second would require an uphill climb of half the distance to the gate, a quarter of a mile, before attaining sight of the demonstrators; and the last would raise the possibility of being caught out of bounds in the woods and would carry greater risk of an escape charge and violence. Clearly, only the first two alternatives are open, and of those two the second, over the fields, would give us enough time to cover ground and make our captors meet us on equal terms, on foot and in sight of the crowd.

"What's tickling you, Red Bear?" Tom from his towering height whispered down at me, "I heard you were all black and snarling after that meeting."

"You heard, eh?" I asked, coming off my bunk.

"Yeah, three or four different ways," Tom said. "Caught David rapping to Tony over in Dorm 5, heard another version from Dan and Beach over in back of 1 and 2. You're stirring the stew, Red Bear. What's up? Here I thought I'd come over and invite you to my place for coffee and a sandwich and get you out of your black mood, and I find you grinning at the wall."

"Yeah, let me get my shoes on and I'll take you up on the sandwich and coffee."

"We'll have to do it in the front corridor. Lights are out in the dorm," he said as we made the corridor of 3 and 4 Dorm. Tom lived now in Dorm 1. He used to live in a cube, but he was busted out of there into The Jungle by a hack who had finally caught him in a violation during a trip to Lewisburg. If a hack wants to bust you, he just waits for the opportunity. This one had waited until Tom was comfortable in his cube. It was a bad bust, too, for it occurred just six months before Tom met the Parole Board, his first trip after five years on a fifteen-year rap for bank robbery.

At his home, cluttered with sports equipment, he got his and his guest's cups out of the locker and made the run for water. I sat in the dark as men rapped on, oblivious to the heavy shapes around them on the beds, heads under pillows, blankets covering all. Unlike Dorm 4 with its cubes, this dorm offered little privacy; and, finding none, no one went out of their way to foster it.

Raps went on after lights out, the movers moved with abandon. Somewhere a bottle clinked against a locker. Maybe Tom could score. Irish coffee would be right, right now.

Tom returned, the steam from the cups of hot water preceding him, fixed the coffee, got the sandwiches from his locker, locked it up, and we were out in the front corridor at a table.

"How's your home?" I asked, knowing the hassles he went through in The Jungle and afterwards, trying and finally succeeding in getting out of it. "You going to make it here?"

"Does a bear shit in the woods?" he said. "I'm not a virgin in this game, Jack. I've taken greater shit than these two-bit hacks can throw at me. It's just a hassle. They know I'm short and they're making it rough, but two can play that game. I've written to Alexander about that bust and I got the doc to write him, too. If that hack isn't pacing the West Street prison soon, I'm a Kamikaze pilot with three missions."

I was staring at the cup before me, so clean, spotless compared with mine. When Tom and I "kept house" together during the first seven months of my bit, he below, I above, in a double bunk in the back corridor of 1 and 2, my tendency to chaos was evident on my locker, books and papers all about, and increasingly evident on his. But he always kept his cups clean, whereas mine gradually turned the color of the coffee made in them.

"So, when are we going to walk, Red Bear?" he asked, breaking my reverie. "I'll be damned if it doesn't make sense to me. All those people on the other side of the fence. No harm to go look at them."

"No harm at all," I laughed. "A little Sunday afternoon stroll. We'll take Mike along. What d'ya think?"

"Sure, Mike, David, you. Anyone else?" he asked.

"Jerry, I think. And if we start, maybe others," I replied.

"What do you think the man is up to? What measures will he take? Any chance of them locking us in?" I had a lot of questions and Tom was a jailwise source of information for me.

"No chance. Visiting day. Besides, they can't show that they're uptight. They'll just keep some hacks down at the gate to check on visitors. Everyone else will be kept outside."

I was feeling lighter and lighter. This fort had suddenly as-

The Walk / 46

sumed the furniture of home (I think Auden once wrote something like that about a bar as World War II started). We ate our sandwiches.

"I see," lifting my half-devoured sandwich, "you're still scoring off of Big Daddy."

"Big Daddy, hell," Tom said. "You mean Sausage. I don't know why he pushes this stuff on me, he's in here now, you know. They were so down on him over in The Jungle, he didn't think he make it much longer. He a pest, an obnoxious pest; but his ham is good."

"Wants protection," I said, finishing the sandwich. "He can't win at cards so frequently, make so many enemies collecting debts, and not have a big man at his back, right?"

"Maybe so," he said. "I've just told him to cool it. If he thinks I'm going to take on half The Jungle for ham sandwiches, I'm a Kamikaze—"

"Yeah, I know, a Kamikaze pilot with three missions," I said, and it was good. We laughed. And then the hack appeared in the hallway to announce the 11 o'clock count. And I hurried off to my own home.

I woke suddenly the next day, like a diver breaking water on his upward surge to air. David was just passing as I came out the door of my dorm. He had half a day's work on the cattle crew in front of him, and I had things to put together.

We picked up our trays, plates, and silverware at the mess hall entrance.

"Hey, good people!" Jerry yelled from the dish-room, bright and beaming behind his garbage pail where he stood to receive the dirty dishes through a window.

"Still on?" Jerry asked.

"Still on," I said.

Nat was at the grill scrambling eggs. Seeing us, he moved to the counter. Mr. Day, the eccentric kitchen hack, turned his back, and Nat filled our plates with steaming scrambled eggs. Had he not been there, Day would have scooped the cold eggs from the pan to give us.

We moved to an empty table in the rear of the room. We got

no response from the other C.O.'s at tables as we passed. In the mess hall the "freeze" is most obviously observed. Not to sit with someone, to move away if the person dummied up on sets his tray on your table, to put distance between you and the unwanted— all of these gestures are ritually carried out for the benefit of the ever-searching eyes of the other prisoners in the mess hall.

David made his scrambled egg sandwich, as he habitually did.

"Tom says he'll walk with us," I began.

"Good," David said. "That makes four."

"I think Mike will go for it, too," I said. "I'll talk to him later. How's the weather over in Number 5?"

"Stormy," he said between bites on his sandwich. "They think it's all an ego-trip on your part."

"If it were an ego-trip, I'd do it myself," I said, conscious of last night's bitterness. I hated this division, the breaking up of our group. I held myself back from thinking about the primary argument I had for the walk: that, after the Chandler issue and the group action we accomplished, we were strong enough now as a group to take this walk in stride.

"Ego-trip," I said bitterly. "Who's on ego-trips, anyway?"

"I know," David said, "I know. Wait, Hobbit, wait. Be patient. Be calm like Sweet Ass Donkey," he continued, referring to his favorite cow.

"Gotta go," he said, as he gathered his plates together and hurried off.

Left alone, I sat and sipped my coffee. The tables of C.O.'s in front of me were not very lively. Heads bowed, they ate silently. I stared and stared as if the backs and sides of their heads had eyes. It was too early to catch Mike. He worked all week on heavy equipment at Project I and slept until the noon meal on Saturday. I decided to go down and lift weights to try to get rid of this energy that stirred within me.

The weight room was empty when I got there. A sign hung above the door and read in crude letters: "The Palace." Above that a horseshoe was nailed. Inside I did not turn the neon lights on, for they revealed the essential dreariness of the place. I preferred the morning sun coming through the windows. Some shadows. It was clean, recently swept, and mopped. Morry must have been down last night.

Morry, the inmate in charge of the weight room, was a forty-five-year-old Jew from upstate New York. He was a "con's con," Tom told me one time. He had been in a Nazi concentration camp during World War II, escaped, came to this country without a dime or a word of English; and, from a junk cart such as one still sees the more resourceful Bowery men push around the Lower East Side of New York City, he built himself a quarter-of-a-million-dollar junk business. Somehow some boxcars of government brass found their way into his yard, and he was now completing his sixth year on a ten-year rap.

Morry taught me how to lift weights; I helped him improve his reading and writing. He was the better teacher and the better student: more patience as a teacher, more seriousness as a student. When I was just beginning to lift, my unused muscles screaming and complaining like abused laborers, he would stop by my house at eight in the morning and almost drag me by the ear or coax me on with half an orange, until I overcame my reluctance, and, cursing the day he was born, I would go with him. Afterwards, the habit formed, and deriving more from the sessions than I cared to admit, I would work out by myself.

Morry kept The Palace clean, stacked and demanded that others stack and put away the weights after using them, There were two benches for press work, an inclining board for sit-ups and more difficult lift exercises, a Preacher's Bench for arm work, chinning bar, and jump ropes, and, of course, bars and weights. Morry was into weight I would never come to lift, although he said I would if I stuck to it. When I reached the point of pressing my own body weight plus ten or twenty pounds, I quit adding to the bars. Forty-five or fifty-pound dumbbells were sufficient, too, for me to exhaust my arms and body in an hour and a half of work—and it was work—after which a hot shower, a cup of coffee, and I was ready for my teaching and whatever tensions or hassles that day might bring.

Morry never made conversation for the sake of conversation, and he was quick to sense my need for silence. His face was lined with his experiences; his eyes, though, were somehow incongruously soft in a frame so muscular: the lines above his

The Walk / 49

eyes formed sensitive, acute angles as they rose deep in the shadowed sockets.

Lifting alone or with Morry served both my mind and body. For after repeatedly concentrating all of my energy on dead weight during an exercise I had to rest afterward, and that pause between exertions, those moments when straining muscles relaxed, were good for my head. Cobwebs and shadows in my mind seemed to disappear with the easing sensation in my arms, shoulders, or chest, and I would pace about or just sit and stare at nothing in particular, my mind sorting and choosing which of its weights to lift next.

On this day, however, there was nothing to sort. I had but one thing on my mind as I assembled the weights and went through with the routine—the walk and how to make it work. If I could count on five men walking, both C.O.'s and regular cons, there was every chance that other C.O.'s would follow. The unknown factor was the nature of the administration's response. The problem: how to avoid any violence.

"Hello, Red Bear," said Sam, my Italian friend, as he strutted into the room. "Working it out, again, eh? I've gotta get to it. Haven't worked out in three days. Getting jittery. Almost offed a guy last night. Makin' noise in the cube next to me. Did ya hear him?" he asked as his shirt came off, revealing his squarely built, thick, and heavy body. At the locker he paused and silently looked at the *Playboy* center-fold pinups taped all over the inside of the door—the beautiful, if somewhat plastic, creatures of the American Dream.

"I'm gonna tear that 'yam' outa there one of these days," he said as he looked intently at a Black nude emerging from a shower.

I thought it was an achievement for *Playboy* to put a Black in its center fold; but a clean Black, drops of moisture clinging to her body, was a bit too much.

Out of the locker Sam took his karate board: a four-by-four piece of wood an inch thick with a small piece of sponge on top and a piece of canvas wrapped around it. He put it on a cement block near one of the benches. With one hand holding the board fast against the block, he drove his fist into the board—one

The Walk / 50

hundred times. The sound of the blows echoed in the small room and drove out all thought.

Finished with his first run, two knuckles of his fist bleeding from the cracked calcium-calloused structures covering them, mini-volcanoes of the karate enthusiasts, weapons really, he looked up and turned his eyes on me.

"Hear you're into something, Red Bear," he said.

"Just a little walk," I said.

"Tom says your guys finked out," he went on. "What's wrong with them? Don't they know they gotta stick together?"

"Well, most of them are sticking together, but not with me," I said.

"Here, let me get that," he said as the weight I was to press wouldn't go up; it was pressing down now on my chest.

"Tom says he likes the idea," he said. "I'm not so sure. These bastards are crazy, ya know. They're capable of anything."

"You wouldn't be interested, would you?" I asked, as I pulled myself up to a sitting position on the bench. And the idea of a contingent of Mafia types walking with us crowded into my head. Sam was the man I spoke to when we needed guys to stay away from the mess hall during the Chandler affair, which included a hunger strike. All of the Italian faction stayed away and were glad to help, for they liked the idea of C.O.'s sticking together. But for them to take this walk to see demonstrators, peace-niks and such, just seemed too much to ask. All the old prejudices would have to be overcome.

"It's an antiprison demonstration," I said. "Not a C.O. thing. It isn't for us; it's for all of us. The first antiprison gathering I've heard about."

"Yeah, I heard that, too. I don't know, Red Bear. We'll wait and see how things are tomorrow. I'll talk to the guys, but won't ask them to do it. Just let it out that we're talking about it, o.k."

"Great," I said, and knowing that was as far as he could go, and realizing I could not keep still in that room any longer, I put my weights away, called out, "Later," and split.

Although it was only ten o'clock in the morning, I could see men already leaving the dorms and heading for the mess hall for lunch, which would begin in fifteen minutes and last until

The Walk / 51

eleven o'clock. It takes considerable time to adjust to prison feeding schedules. If a body is not careful, he finds himself eating on the early chow lines, and that means eating all three meals between the hours of 6:30 A.M. and 3:30 P.M. Hunger at nine at night can be almost traumatic: emptiness within and without. Hence the need all prisoners have to stash a part of a meal in a "tote" bag inside a shirt or coat and carry it back to the dorm for a nine o'clock snack.

I stopped to fill my pipe. The sun bore down and sweat poured out of me. I closed my eyes to it and behind the lids a scarlet field appeared with a white hot ball in the center.

I knew I had time to take a shower, contact Mike, and, together with Tom, make the tail end of the chow line.

The idea of Sam and maybe twenty or more Italians joining us in the walk was a little too much to think about. It was one thing to ask them to refrain from eating a meal in support of C.O.'s; it was quite another to expect that they join in such a demonstration. I suspected that the possibility of violence would be proportionate to the numbers involved: serious danger of it with one or two; probable with five or six; less as the numbers rose; none at all if thirty or forty showed up. The administration would be faced with more than it could handle openly, and it would be forced to accommodate them—perhaps even permitting them, out of pseudo generosity, to greet the demonstrators at the gate, as they already had granted an entertainment event for this afternoon.

What fellowship would then be accomplished! Prisoners—hard-core con, Mafia types, C.O.'s—all greeting peace people at a prison gate, all opposed to prisons, all done in the face of the jailers. Too much.

I doubted that that would ever be, though, as much as the possibility might be within reach. The clannishness of the Italian group—based on survival and personal advancement within jail and acting frequently in opposition to inmates as well as administrators, was something that might be overcome by an issue more central to their concerns than an antiprison demonstration. Yet what could be more central than to act in opposition to the prison in which they as well as we were held?

I knew, too, that it was out of my hands: I could not speak of it to any other Italian, that was Sam's role; and, as he said, it would depend on what was happening Sunday afternoon. Nor could I speak, even were I able to gather them together, to the C.O.'s; I did not know how they would respond to a Mafia-type contingent. There were prejudices on both sides. As a group we were as much a faction, as much into our thing for our interests, ego and otherwise, as the Italians were a faction and into their interests. The idea appealed to me, though, because it would amount to overcoming factionalism, walking a high road above ego-trips. Right now there existed enough factionalism to break an organizer's heart. The C.O.'s were distrustful of me; I, of them: so goes the "freeze." And none of us was involved (beyond Sam's play and Mike and Tom's willingness to walk) with other groups within the prison.

Mike, Tom, and I were not about to miss lunch. In at the side entrance of the Administration building, we took the steps to the hallway three at a time and goose-stepped past the control center, where prisoners were being shaken down for visits, the caseworker's office, the commissary, and the superintendent's office, all locked up on weekends, and into the entrance of the mess hall. We were the last in line. That meant we might have to eat hurriedly, but there would be more to eat. For the food already on the counter would be distributed to all comers and we were the first, being last, of the comers. Men from the tables were heading in haste toward the counter as the call, "More chops!" went up, and we moved away, grinning like kids, our plates overflowing with pork chops, pie on top of pie, bowls of lettuce salad—a once a week item—vegetables, and hot rolls. Not to get what you can out of the kitchen, or to miss the infrequent good meals, served with visitors to the camp in mind, is considered sheer stupidity by the jailwise. When we scored in such a way, we were not grateful to the State for our plateful of goodies: we knew the officials could not care less about our diet and could order a meal both nourishing and well prepared whenever it served their own interest. Rather, increased contempt was directed toward the State. We were simply taking what they owed us, partial payment for the pain they caused us. Were prisons not, in fact, long-term uninhabitable homes, such poor manners on the part of these wayward sons would not be needed.

Both Tom and Mike were athletes: Tom a tennis and golf amateur of high standing, Mike a boxer and softball player. Tom was coaching and managing the camp softball team on which Mike filled the catcher's spot. Wise in the ways of jail, they used their ability in sports to gain access to the outside. Teams must play other teams on the latter's fields. So the camp's team was frequently on trips out of the camp to play in neighboring towns. But both men were aware of how they were being used by the very system they as prisoners attempted to exploit. A good softball team is good public relations for a prison, and Tom was sent to Allenwood expressly to handle the sports scene and build tennis courts as he did at Lewisburg and Atlanta. Mike, on his part, was normally not a minimum security risk. But he knew and could operate heavy machinery and Project I needed such a man. If they were being manipulated, however, they could manipulate in turn. They seldom missed a score. But it was a nervous time for both because they were soon to face the Parole Board, each for the first time, and the Parole Board is one of the foremost occasions of pain in a prisoner's life: by its nature it fosters Hope, "rotten-thighed Hope," as Kazantzakis wrote of it.

But at that table in the rear of the mess hall all went well; a banquet mood prevailed. We evaluated the pork chops, distributed the large and small ones among us, and commented on each chop's individual good points or lack of them; the lettuce was not as fresh as it might have been but there was abundance, if not quality; the vegetables were, as usual, canned and tasteless; the pie, as usual, was mostly cornstarch; but the Kool-Aid, the Kool-Aid, for some reason, was just right. Talk about the walk seemed superfluous. We all were of one mind. It was the thing to do. "To hell with the motherfuckers!" Mike said. We ate as if it were the last meal before a battle.

There was really little to do now but wait. Whenever in jail I became conscious of waiting, and that was often, I remembered Kenneth Patchen's poem about a man in jail for murder. The poem consisted of the one word "wait" repeated at intervals, space surrounding each repetition, all over the clean white page. To those who have never been inside a jail, that experience must appear to be one long wait—to get out. But it is really never that simple, as Patchen knew; rather it is a series without order, yet nonetheless a series, of variegated, multicolored waits of varying degrees of intensity or pettiness. Intense might be the wait for the Parole Board; petty, the wait for the noonday count, which was our next wait after devouring lunch. Nothing could be done until that occurred. But, so petty a wait, for one with something to do, was intense; and the intense waits, for one without hope, were petty and pointless.

Neither intense nor petty in the usual sense was the wait before me now; rather it was as if I were waiting for a rain, a rain that will come in its own time. There was nothing more I could do but wait. To lose patience with clouds is absurd. Perhaps I could allay any fears David and Jerry might have of violence; but, since I did not have any more of a clue, beyond jailwise conjectures, than they of the official response, I could not feel comfortable in doing that. Yet, on a walk early that afternoon before the entertainment, sponsored by the groups that organized the demonstration, I found myself saying to David and Jerry that there was little violence to be feared. I was sad that I lacked David's enthusiasm—his face shined—and I was disquieted because I could not tell them of Sam and the possibility of an Italian contingent. I was certain, however, the walk would go off, somehow, someway; and though the danger was real, I could not believe that it would be such that we could not handle it.

Tossed between glee and sadness, as I shared either in David's joy or Jerry's fears, compounded by my own bittersweet reflections on the event to take place tomorrow, I and my friends found seats in the hall of the Education building and waited for the entertainment to begin.

If the organized, ritualized ceremonies of institutionalized religion find few adherents on the street in our time, such is true to an even greater degree in jail, where few men (except

The Walk / 55

the Jehovah's Witnesses, the simple folk, and the Amish, the sincere folk) freely exhibit any religious bent. Those who do are commonly and justifiably looked upon with scorn. To use the chaplain's clerk position or to get tight with the chaplain himself, while affecting a religiosity as contrived as his, is looked upon by hard core as the apex of phoniness, the least honorable of hustles. The huge bus that carried prisoners to Sunday services never contained more than four men. To a large extent, the religious forces as they existed in the prison were found by men, alone or in groups, in music.

The Blacks have jazz, soul, and hard rock; the Puerto Ricans, bongo drums and Spanish guitar; the Italians, an opera hour Sunday evenings in Number 5 dorm; the hillbillies, country-western on AM radio; the C.O.'s and druggies, rock, folk, and blues. All groups have their own music that articulates for them their culture and roots, gives expression to their despair and hopes, and arouses in them emotions that are at once each man's and that of the group of which he's a part. Music, not divine worship, created what unity existed within a group. Music, not formulated prayer, overcame ego-trips and rigidity, broke down barriers and un-isolated men. But not completely. The Italian opera hour was not open to all comers; Black soul music beat with strange tensions if others than Blacks wanted to stay in the music room; few ever accepted, as might be expected, the J.W.'s invitation to their prayer and hymn service Sunday afternoons; and C.O.'s lost some of their spontaneity if non-C.O.'s witnessed their vulnerability to rock, folk, and the blues. Some men, deeply into blues and jazz, could cross barriers. Dickey Wiley and Alex, both performers as well as listeners, could move freely among Blacks, and some of the guitar-playing C.O.'s could jam with the hillbillies.

Musical entertainment for the whole population was not, therefore, simply entertainment. It involved the common source of unity among prisoners. This afternoon's entertainment was no exception. In fact, one of the performers, whose name was mentioned on the official notice announcing the event, was a Black minister. A comedian and a woman vocalist and guitarist were also on the show.

Known to some of the C.O.'s and Black resisters, the minister had been with Martin Luther King in Mississippi, Georgia, and other places of confrontation. He and Pete Seeger carried civil rights, peace, and anti-government songs into many demonstrations, prisons, colleges, and on tour throughout the 1960's. A man of great stature, of enormous energy, a veritable John Henry incarnate, he filled the small hall with his presence and his sounds. The authentic blues of Mississippi and Georgia, Freedom songs, and rich sounds of brotherhood against oppression, echoed in the hall and seemed to linger long after a song had ended. He seemed inexhaustible: a deep, dark well of sorrow, sacrifice, joy, and pain.

Laughter—the rich, earthy, gut sound of body agreeing with mind—was provided by the comedian, a man with a similar background as the minister. We laughed to see the foundations of our experience in jail—cops, hacks, administrators, cells, laws, and need—lifted before our eyes, looked at askance, and—clearly no longer threats—tossed off, swept under our laughter and the comedian's drawling country tones.

The young and attractive vocalist translated the vibrations she was receiving from the hungry, horny audience before her and gave us lullabies so soft and soulful that, as the show ended, we were not conscious of being deprived so much as of being refreshed and nourished.

Nat and Johnny, sitting in front of us, were well into it all, the C.O.'s around us were high on good vibrations; but, standing in the rear of the hall, Tommy and some of his friends seemed uptight, defensive, and angry.

Once outside the hall, however, after the inmates had poured out in a rush to reach the mess hall early or their homes, as a bowl is emptied of its contents, the libation spilled upon the ground, so the enthusiasm and emotion provoked by the show seemed to disappear, to dissipate, as singly or in threes and fours men went separately to their destinations.

By nine o'clock that evening I was conscious of two disintegrating forces at work: the first was the bad vibrations coming from Sam and the Italians, who were (I surmised) disturbed by the pro-Black music and mood of the entertainment. There

The Walk / 57

seemed to be little fellowship with the clan at this point. The organizers of the demonstration, who were in contact with the C.O.'s through visiting, all legal and authorized by the administration, held on weekends for friends of prisoners, taking their cue from the C.O.'s suggestion that the event not be limited to prisoners of conscience, had evidently chosen entertainers who would sing to a wider audience: The Blacks and country-western folk in particular. But what does one sing to the Mafia? And who, in the planning stages of the event, would have had the Mafia in mind anyway?

The second disintegrating force was the rumors coming out of the kitchen and from men recently at Lewisburg that spoke of hyper-sensitive administrators, and super-paranoid security measures in the face of tomorrow's action. Not forty but sixty additional hacks were being talked about; kitchen men had had to prepare lunches for them. Federal agents moving among the people, talk of a riot squad or the "goon" squad from Lewisburg being on call, and again talk of locking all prisoners inside the dorms in the afternoon—all rumors; but rumors are swallowed whole where certainty is wanting.

After the nine o'clock count, a little anxious and disturbed, I went in search of Tom in 1 and 2 Dorm. I found, not Tom, but Bob Eaton, Bill Boss, John Bach, and one or two other C.O.'s who wanted to talk about the walk. So there, in the corridor, as prisoners passed between us on the way to the TV room, I told them how the thing looked, those already interested (neglecting to mention Tommy and his group), and we got into a long rap on how we could do it and what we could expect from the hacks and administrators. By count time eight other C.O.'s, plus Tom, Mike, Jerry, David, and myself, were ready.

Sunrise over Penny Hill on Sunday morning. Mild and meek it was, too: gentle blues streaked with rose and the promise of bright yellows. So were we mild and meek, half-awake, half in touch with today's and yesterday's dreams. The sunrise did not last, nor did our mild mood. The sun, fully advanced into the sky upon our leaving the mess hall after breakfast, seemed to cling to every object in our sight, enhance its lines with brightness; even as we, now fully awake to our prison world again, saw with clarity, if not composure, the traces of this day's activities taking place, as the innumerable impressions of unusual activity on the part of hacks combined with the rumors already in our minds to force upon us a need for concentration out of rhythm with the haste and movement taking place before us.

"Let us go and look at the cows," David said.

And we did. And never were the cows more content with the grass of a prison pasture, more voluntarily dependent upon it, more docile in their chewing, more calm as they raised their heavy heads to turn and watch us watching them. They were so content to be unfree; so compliant in captivity. The sun in its upward climb gave forth more heat; the Hereford colors, red and white, were brilliant on a field of green; and that fire in the sky seemed to make the cows cling closer to the earth and each other. They gave up feeding, settled down, and spread their bulk upon the ground.

Back in camp, Bob Eaton, Bill Boss, John Bach, Dickey Wiley, and Jerry Foster were all gathered around Eaton's bunk in Number 5 Dorm, discussing the latest rumors and news.

"Have you seen all the new hacks around?" Bill Boss asked.

"They're cruising around, two to a truck, crisscrossing all around the camp," said Eaton. "They're afraid the hippie-long-hairs will come over the fence everywhere."

"Someone said they saw a shotgun in Engle's station wagon," Wiley said. "I can't believe that he's that stupid."

"If you stand over in the parking lot you can hear the loud-speakers," Jerry said. "They must be setting up over there. The hacks shooed me away."

"Wonder how many will show?" Eaton asked.

David and I found seats on the opposite bunk and listened. Everyone was excited, smiling. All the bad tensions were gone. The vibrations were all good.

"My man McKinnis," said Bill Boss, "is the man in charge of the Administration building today. And he looks it. Man, is he worried."

"Bogie is staked out at Education," John Bach said.

"Hey, Jack," said Eaton. "John and I thought it would be good if we went down the road dressed like the 'Spirit of '76' with drum, fife, and flag. We can make a peace flag out of a sheet. Someone has a flute that'll do. We can play 'Yankee Doodle' on it . . ."

"Yeah, and a trash can can be our drum," said John.

"Sounds good to me," I said.

"Let's do it, then," cried Dickey. "What a scene that'll be!"

"I'll wear the bandage," Jerry said.

"I got the drum!" cried David.

"I'll play the flute," Eaton said. "I think I can learn 'Yankee Doodle' by—when? When are we going to march?" he asked.

"I should think between one and two," I said. "Can't be any later than two or two-thirty, and if we moved earlier we might upset whatever they're doing. A guy from Bucknell at the entertainment yesterday said they were still talking about coming through the gate."

"Between one and two, then," said Eaton. "Who's going to get a flag?"

"I'll get it," said Bill Boss. "I've got a pole, too."

No sign of hesitancy or uncertainty existed among those gathered. All the roles were divided up. I felt like a guest at my own party. But the feelings were all good. I looked around at the dreary dorm. Dan was pouring over his newspaper, his bunk still in shadows. He had to know; no need for invitations. There was still time.

David was rocking back and forth, the light in his eyes beaming on all of us. The group broke up to seek bandage, fife, drum, and flag; others went to scout on the hacks' activities. The parking lot in front of the Administration building had been crawling with hacks all morning; they seemed to be enjoying themselves; frequently one would pause, as he stood on the floor of his pickup truck before getting in, to shout something to another: John Wayne in his jeep.

I still had to contact Tom and Mike, whom I had not seen all morning. But I could not find Tom or Mike anywhere. And I

The Walk / 60

decided that that was how they wanted it. I could not force a meeting, and I could not blame them, in the face of upcoming Parole Board meetings and these super-paranoid security measures. It was obvious that the administrators were not concerned about appearing uptight, as Tom had suggested. But the idea of the family that had kept this walk alive, that it should break apart and never come together; that idea was a keen disappointment to me. I knew, too, if I continued to seek them at a time when they did not wish to be found, that I would succeed only in alienating them. It was best, I thought, to let it be. "Those'll go who'll go," as David had said.

Influenced by Tom's and Mike's response, as I read it, to the security measures, I began to think seriously of our predicament should they in fact lock us in after the noon count. It would be easy enough to shout to each other from windows in the dorms. All three dorms could communicate in that way. And, should they lock us in, I was all for going over the wall at an agreed time. It would be easy enough to do; the old dorm, Number 5 or The Jungle, could not be locked anyway. And the two new dorms were only one story high with flat roofs; men bent on contraband late at night frequently resorted to going out over the wall. It would mean that we never got to walk, but the end would be the same. Considerably more dangerous though. And without prior discussion perhaps it would never find willing men to do it. I would be right back where I was Friday evening.

While thinking of these things on my return to my home for the noon count, I accidentally ran into Tom.

"There's a lot of movement going on, Jack," he said. "I saw Hendricks and Rauch in the parking lot. Hendricks left with Engle in the station wagon. They're parked down at the cross-roads. You'd never make it down the road."

"Yes, I know. It looks tighter and tighter," I said. "We've got some C.O.'s interested now. Looks like a good group. I'm even thinking of going over the wall should they lock us in."

"That's a little much," Tom said.

"Yes, a little much. Let's hope it doesn't come to that."

"I'll see you later, Red Bear," he said and his long legs carried him off quickly. I knew then that he wouldn't be going with us, but we both understood why and it was okay.

Back in my cube for count, I watched for Sam in his cube on the other side in the middle of the dorm. When the hack called, "Count," Sam rose, but unlike our usual game of waving and exchanging greetings, his back was turned to me. I knew then it would be a mistake to confront him. He was telling the other Italians in the dorm, by this gesture, that the C.O. action was not on for them. So it goes.

The house and some of the family that Jack built seemed to be crumbling. But there was still the walk with David and Jerry. And there were the other good men willing to do it. The "Spirit of '76" was a damn good idea. I wish I had though of it. Count was cleared over the bitch box. They were not going to lock us in.

I went out into the midday sun. The bright yellow disk bore down from above. Men stayed under the porches rather than move out into it. A haze seemed to move around the edges of the compound.

I decided to check out the rumor I heard that Bogie, one of the hacks, was stationed down at the Education building. Coming back from a walk, Dan met me on the road near Industries.

"So, you're going through with it," he said.

"Yes, I think it's a good thing," I replied.

"A fucking death trip," he said angrily. "Why don't you save your energy for something useful?" he asked.

"Utility isn't my bag," I said. "Folly is."

"Well, what you're doing is foolish all right. Dangerous, too."

"We'll see," I said. And aware that Bogie was indeed making himself visible and important I returned to Dorm 4.

Enthusiasm was high outside as C.O.'s gathered around the porch. Eaton was practicing "Yankee Doodle," on his flute. Jerry was playing with his ketchup-stained bandage. David squatted on the stoop, his trash can between his legs. Other C.O.'s were congregated, in an obviously nonchalant manner, underneath the bitch box, attached to the roof of the dorm some twenty feet away, in full view, as we all were, of the hacks in the control center. The bitch box carried the walkie-talkie

The Walk / 62

broadcasts that were being made by cruising hacks and station-wagoned administrators as they guarded their prison from the invaders.

I sat and beat time with an eager foot to the improvising of Eaton on the flute and David on the drum. Alex, who was a drummer, took over David's sound and up-tempoed the rendition. Wiley was weaving back and forth, his wild blond hair keeping time, as he squatted cross-legged on the grass.

"They just caught a longhair hippie!" shouted Billy "the librarian" from underneath the bitch box. "He came over the fence on the other side of Penny Hill."

"Great! Let 'em all come over!" yelled David.

"What are they going to do with him?" Eaton asked.

"Just put him back," replied Billy. "They checked it out with Hendricks and Engle. 'Calling Allenwood I. Calling Allenwood I. Come in, Allenwood I,'" and Billy mocked the tones of the call to the administrators at the crossroads.

"Big fucking deal. Our great men at work," sneered Jerry.

"In-fucking-deed," said John Bach. "All they're doing is giving the hacks a high."

The music changed. A solemn march on the drum with delicate accompaniment of the flute. A sudden shift in mood overcame us. Though still high, we were quieter about it. Jerry began a pantomime and was joined by David, who held a playing card in one outstretched hand.

Suddenly, over the bitch box came the sound: "Eaton, No. 35906, report to control center. You have a visit. Eaton, No. 35906, report to the control center. You have a visit."

"Who is that, Bob?" I asked.

"Didn't you have a visit yesterday?" asked Jerry. "Man, wish I could get visits like that."

"It must be my mother," said Eaton.

"Well, what's it going to be? Are you still in on the walk?" John asked.

"Sure, I'll just ask her to leave by two o'clock. At the latest, two-thirty. Will that be okay?"

"Why not?" I said. "Two is good with us. Hey, David, what's

the card all about?" I asked.

"Oh, that. Dan gave it to me," he said. "It's the ace of spades."

I went back to my cube. Another hour or more remained. I would have a cup of coffee.

"Want some water, Jack?" Nat asked as I came into the cube.

"Yeah, just what I need," I said.

"You seem kinda nervous already. Maybe you should have some hot chocolate instead," Nat said.

"I'm okay," I said. "We're going for a little walk in a while. Shouldn't miss it."

"A walk? I heard something about it. Didn't know it was still on," he said. "You're going on it?"

"Yeah, I'm on it," I said.

"My man!" Nat said grinning. "I'll buy your coffee," and he made my coffee. "Gotta go and fix the meat for tomorrow. I'll be watching. When is it to go?" he asked.

"Sometime after two," I said.

"Great. Good luck," and he moved away, handsome in pressed kitchen whites, a blue handkerchief tied around his neck.

I needed the coffee, but more than that I needed time and a place to think—away from the distractions.

The walk was certain to take place. I was convinced it was the right thing to do. Despite Dan. Bring the prisoners to the people. It was right for them; right for us. I remembered then the Christmas Eves I'd spent singing carols on the sidewalk before the Women's House of Detention in New York's West Village. The small group of Catholic Workers and others had been doing it each year since the late 1940's. The tall dark building rose mournfully amid the neon lights of the bars and stores surrounding it. All the windows had bars and grates. On the sidewalk where we stood, huddled against the cold, last-minute Christmas shoppers were scurrying home, hailing taxis, thinking about presents. . . . And all the huge black building was filled with women away from home, kids, husbands. So we would sing. We'd sing all the traditional carols—the only ones we knew off the top of our heads, and the unsteady sounds of our untrained voices went up into the darkness. Then we would hear the faint voices of the women locked behind the bars high in the shadows. Handkerchiefs would appear at some places. Shouts for a favorite carol would come down. We would try to sing it and strain to keep in time with the distant sounds, the small thin voices through cracks in windows coming from above.

Yes, it would be good for us. Good, too, for the bloody prison system. We would be providing a real definition, should any administrator need one, of prisoners: not powerless pawns in administrative games, in which all the rules are formulated by guidelines, procedures, and whims of officials; but reluctant rebels, always capable of saying "Fuck it!" to the whole mess, walking out of it, not substantially altered by the system, not the products of the United States Federal Prison System, as the labels on the lockers, made in prison industries, read: "We produce furniture and men."

This walk into the "hole" would mean that I would not get parole. But I had made it clear to the Parole Board, when I went before them in November, that I had not altered my principles nor would change my life style as a result of prison or in anticipation of parole. And I knew I could not survive on the street, leashed to some probation officer, for six months or more. That special favor I would not accept. It is a good way to get out of this cube, too. Enough of special favors.

Besides, the "hole" was fascinating. I felt obligated to experience it. Allenwood was too much of a country club. A ranch, as Tony said. Why not be a guest of Hendricks, Rauch, and Parker? Let's see what they've got. What their secrets are. It was humiliating to remain under the threat of the "hole" and not really know what the "hole" was all about.

The catch is getting into the "hole." One can be busted for all kinds of things. Foolish mistakes, absurd risks. It is best if we go in on our own terms. What more radical way of getting busted is there than to get busted walking out of jail? Beats sitting down, I thought. Their pipe dream come true. Yes.

Thus do lawbreakers behave. Laws are but the limitations of small men's minds. Jailed for breaking laws of the State, we break the laws of the jail. Proving we are still free even in fetters.

As all men should be. And without blame. Without blame.

"Hey, Jack," said John as he hurried into my cube. "Something's come up."

"What is it?" I asked.

"Mrs. Eaton wants to walk with us," he said.

"She what!" I shouted.

"Bob's mother. She wants to go on the walk with us. They're up in front of the visiting room now. It's almost two-thirty . . ."

"How can she walk with us?" I asked, and I did not know how to handle this thing. "How can we do it? Where would we start?"

"I don't know," said John, as perplexed as I by this twist. "I just know she wants to walk."

"Can you find out any more?" I asked. "Find out how she thinks we can pull it off? What's Bob think?"

"I'll try," John said, and I followed him out of the dorm. He went straight up to the lawn in front of the visiting room and talked with Mrs. Eaton and Bob. Surely, it's a strange fucking day, I thought. Are the hacks going to permit that?

The groups around the porch and under the bitch box were silent, wondering what was happening.

"What's up?" asked David.

"Mrs. Eaton wants to walk with us," I said.

"Oh," he said. That was my response too. How to handle this scene? If we tried for the road with fife (but Eaton's got the fife), drum, and flag, it would mean Mrs. Eaton would have to cross the hill down the road—we would have to run for it anyway. With her? But with Engle down there, the road is out anyway. They would stop her before she got out of the yard. John was returning.

"She says she's going to start from the sidewalk there," he said.

"Well, what are we supposed to do? Follow her down the road to Education? That's in the wrong direction," and I was almost screaming.

"What is Bob going to do?" I asked.

"He's going to stay with his mother," John said.

"Oh, great," I said.

"Well, when are they going to do this?" I asked.

The Walk / 66

"Soon, I guess," John said, his sensitive features showing the strain.

"Well, see if you can find out exactly when. If they leave from the front, we can go out the back. Find out if you can, okay?"

It looked as if the fife, drum, and flag business would be lost. We would have to leave by the back door of this dorm, go around the rear of the Administration building, and into the fields. If Mrs. Eaton and Bob went out the front way, that might keep the hacks inside busy enough for us to get a head start.

I did not see Mrs. Eaton or Bob. Someone told me they went into the visiting room. I wondered what was happening now. How could they leave from there? Which way? Out the side entrance? It was a little too much. If she went out the side entrance, we could meet her in the parking lot and go over the side down to the road and then into the fields on the other side.

"Man, this is confusing," said Jerry. "What's happening?"

"Are we going to walk or not?" asked David.

There seemed to be fewer C.O.'s around than before. It was getting late, close to three o'clock. I suggested we all go to the rear of the dorm and wait there for John. I wondered if he'd be back. How would he get into and out of the visiting room, since he didn't belong there or have a visit?

We had just arrived at the rear of the dorm when Dickey Wiley came running up to us. He had been sitting under the bitch box.

"They just told Hendricks and Engle that you all left the front porch," he said.

"What do we do now?" asked Dickey. We were all nervous.

"Wait for John," I said.

"Looks like I won't need my bandage," said Jerry.

"Won't need this drum either," said David.

Just then John came striding, tall and graceful, around the corner of the TV room. Bill Boss was behind him, his guitar in his hand.

The Walk / 67

"We gotta go, if we're going," he said.

"Well, let's go," I said.

"Wait!" Jerry shouted. "There's a truck coming this way." And from the direction of the softball field a pickup truck, two hacks aboard, was speeding toward us. We closed the door and stood inside and watched as it approached.

"You can't take that guitar with you," I said to Bill Boss, my voice edgy. He turned red. He was shaking his guitar above his head.

"I'll take what I goddamned like on this damn thing! And you aren't going to tell me anything!" he screamed as he shoved me away. I shut up. What was happening anyway?

"Truck's gone," Jerry said.

"Let's go," said John, leading the way, his face suddenly serious. David grasped my hand. We joined Jerry as he went through the door; and, suddenly, we were on the road under the sun and moving.

John was striding straight down the middle of the road, stately, dignified, like a priest in procession. Wiley, a freaked-out altar boy in his dirty kitchen whites, seemed to be going in all directions at once: arms, legs, head all moving to his own weird rhythm. David, Jerry, and I, walking abreast and quickly to keep up with John, broke out laughing at the two in front of us, one graceful, the other spastic. Bill Boss was behind us. We reached the rear of the Administration building, turned the corner, and there at the crossroads some distance off was the black station wagon with Engle and Hendricks in it. There was a thick wood that ran along the upper edge of the field we were about to enter. It formed sort of the back side of Penny Hill. For all we knew super-hacks were hiding behind the trees.

But we did not want to go too far down that road, so we turned off and scrambled down and then up the drainage ditch by the roadside, and made the crest of the embankment. A barbed wire fence, the boundary of the compound, was before us. John had reached it and stood waiting for the rest of us to make the climb.

"Go on," I said. "We're here." And John stepped over the fence with ease. I stopped to consider it a second and decided to leap it. David and Jerry were beside me. "Let's go," I said and took the distance in a couple of strides and was in the air. At that moment, or just as I landed on the other side, I was aware of the black station wagon starting up down at the crossroads, heard some yelling from the parking lot, and discovered such strength in my legs, such a surge of energy all directed forward—"Rip it off!"—that I had to tell myself not to run. "Walk! Walk! Walk!" I kept shouting to myself. Yet I wanted to run; I needed to run. "Long John is gone"—the words of an old chain gang song came to me, over and over. I was high. David was hopping on my right. Jerry, grinning, was taking long strides on my left. John, taller than all of us, was ten feet in front. The going was not easy: the field had been plowed, not for crops, but for some construction purposes. Earth had been rolled up like breakers and we had to jump over them, still trying to keep it at a walk. Run—and they might shoot, the stupid bastards.

"Someone shouted my name to stop," Jerry yelled.

And we heard then a loud voice from a megaphone: "Stop. I order you all to stop and return to the compound. You are out of bounds. Stop! This is an order."

We kept going. On the road to our left trucks were moving in both directions. They'll try and cut us off, I thought.

"Hey, hacks are running after us," Jerry shouted. I did not want to look around. We were well into the field. We still had the top of the hill to make. And we still could not see the demonstrators. We heard them, though. Someone was making a speech. I hoped, and I heard my voice on Friday evening, that they at least see us getting busted. One damn long walk, I thought. All these waves to leap over. We were beyond the final mound of plowed earth and approaching the crest of the hill. A single line of young trees running down to the road and what used to be a stone fence marked the top. I heard then the hacks behind. They were closing in. Jerry was off some ten yards to my left, David and Dickey were just behind me, John still up front and moving. I didn't see Bill Boss.

John made the crest of the hill and turned around. At that

point, Jerry was tackled by a huge hack who just threw himself over Jerry, more it seemed out of exhaustion than to pinion his legs. The hacks had been running.

"Stop!" I shouted to John, who had begun to move again.

"No, let's go on," he said.

"Jerry's down," I shouted. "Let's stay here."

Two other hacks grabbed David and Dickey and twisted their arms behind their backs. That was all of the hacks from behind. I stood and waited for the two puffing figures coming toward me now from the front. I was exhilarated. Yet, it was so strange. There I was standing still. I was waiting to be captured. Breathing was loud all around. Jerry was up, his arm now twisted behind him. I recognized one of the hacks approaching. It was Mr. Stretch, a young and as yet unhardened hack. The other was a monster from Lewisburg. Stretch saw me and moved ahead of his partner. He came up and took my arm with a show, if nothing more, of anger and moved away from the other hack, who went off to get John, standing not far away.

I felt a little silly as I stood there, my arm now pinioned. Mr. Stretch waited for John's hack to come up to us. Dickey, Jerry, and David were all being led off. They looked back and I waved. It was all very funny, I thought. We could see the crowd from where we stood. We did not know if they saw us. The crowd looked like any other crowd, doing what crowds do. They seemed oblivious to the little sideshow on the hilltop. No matter. These woods were new to me—and I realized I had never seen these woods before, nor looked at the camp from this direction before. The whole thing is utterly new, I thought. Even the mountain seemed strange.

The Hole

There was little to do now but yield to the inevitable. There they were on the road behind the Administration building. Rauch, Hendricks, Engle, the hacks, and the station wagons. Mr. Stretch and I, Mr. Monster and John, joined the others. Rauch gave orders for the disposition. Jerry, John, and I, plus Mr. Stretch and Mr. Monster, were in one station wagon. David, Dickey, and two more hacks, one from Allenwood, one from Lewisburg, in the other.

"Take them out the back gate," said Rauch.

"Are you okay?" I asked Jerry in the back seat of the station wagon.

"Yeah, I'm fine," he said, rubbing his wrist. John was silent on the other side of him. We were all thinking now about Lewisburg, the "hole," what we were soon to experience. We had felt, for the first time, the hands of hacks. Now we were about to be taken into the huge walled-in and turreted prison, the house of evil, their home ground.

The station wagon was moving. We could see some of the inmates running along the path from the Administration building toward Number 5 Dorm. They were waving and shouting. I could not recognize any of them. As we drove down the pasture road we passed Tom as he jogged back toward the camp. He did not look very happy. I saw him scan the car without appearing to, gave him the peace sign, and then caught the words of the Lewisburg hack in front.

"Better call the rear gate. Tell 'em we got escapees coming in. Been a riot out here," he said, not hiding a certain pleasure as he said the words "escapee" and "riot." Stretch made the call.

I looked at Mr. Monster. He filled easily half of the front

seat; his great bulk prevented any view out the front window; his huge hairy paw and arm were resting on the top of the back-rest. He wore a silver ring with an eagle and flag mounted on it. He looked like every young boy's picture of a football coach. Hard lines, close-cropped hair, square jaw, peaked nose, small calculating eyes. He resembled a type of superior workingman, a carpenter or cabinetmaker, I had met a few times in working-men's bars. They were good men to drink with. Expert on the shuffleboard. Loud earthy laughter came from them. They had a great capacity for play. But, try as I might, I could not fit him in, or, rather, he consistently struggled out of the bags I would put him in. Again and again he would mention "riot" and "escape" to Stretch. And, more disturbing than that, he kept glancing back to where I sat, his small intense eyes never moving above my crotch. Bloody latent, I thought. And I yearned for that cell in the hole with a heavy door locking out everything. If we could only flow unhassled into the hole, beyond the rear gate and out of reach of this gay cop, we'll make it, I told myself.

On Rt. 15 and heading toward Lewisburg, we passed through the small town of Allenwood: a post office, gas station, some unpainted clapboard houses. Life in all his everyday ways was cutting his lawn. We passed a hippie-longhair hitching toward Allenwood. Jerry gave him the peace sign. We drove past the Reptile Farm. Bad omen, perhaps. I wondered if Engle took his self-image from that cobra on the sign.

I wanted to smoke my pipe. Then I remembered the pipe tool, a small pocketknife type of instrument, that a friend of mine smuggled into prison for me. It was in my pocket. They would discover it when they frisked us at the rear gate. I wondered if I should try to stuff it between the rear and seat cushions of the car. I really hated to lose it. But it obviously was contraband, street-stuff. We turned off the highway and into the back road leading to the rear gate of Lewisburg. Beautiful countryside around here. Hills and pasture, Angus cows, sheep. And sud-denly, looming before us, was the tall, long, red-brick wall of Lewisburg, turrets at either end. We could see the hacks inside the turret, behind the green glass. They were watching us with binoculars.

The Hole / 74

What had been in my mind a dark abyss took on most concrete proportions. The mammoth square structure the size of a medieval city, complete with an arch and iron gate, was before us. The three of us looked at it, looked at each other: kids about to plunge into the quarry pool. The other station wagon pulled up behind us. They opened the rear fence gate, a prelude to the iron gate, and the cars went in. Five huge hacks were waiting in a semicircle. Mr. Stretch and Mr. Monster got out and slammed the doors. The hacks from the rear car got out. I saw that the one from Allenwood was Mr. Stoned, one of the alcoholics. They banged on the windows for us to get out. Jerry followed John out one side and joined David and Dickey; I went out on my side, still holding the pipe tool in my hand in my pocket. All the hacks were up front now, the two Allenwood hacks, with their backs to the inmates by the side of the car, were talking to the goon squad. I had to pass them as I went in front of the car to join my friends.

"These guys are okay," said Mr. Stoned in a low voice.

"They won't give you any trouble," Mr. Stretch said softly. "Nonviolent types."

And I came together with the others. We were glad to be together, smiled and grabbed at each other. Why only in fairy tales is Mordor wrapped in dark clouds and shadows? Everything around us was clear and bright. I was impressed with the brickwork of the arch. Behind us the sun reflected off the tops of barns far away. The hills were green. There was no haze at all.

"Okay, line up," we heard someone growl. One of the hacks squared off in front of me, an old meerschaum pipe in his mouth. Not bad. He felt in my pockets, examined my pipe and pouch, ran his hands up my legs, around my belt, slapped my thighs, and with a motion of his head urged me over. He had missed the pipe tool. The others were frisked by other hacks. Wiley could hardly stand still for it, but he was joking with his man.

"Back in the cars," they ordered. Inside again, we waited for the hack in the turret above by the arch to lower the huge key to the iron gate. It came down jerkily on a rope. The gate opened with harsh, grating sounds and we moved into the yard of the prison. I was relieved. Let's keep flowing, I said to myself.

The Hole / 75

We passed the huge tree, the only tree in the yard, and it was alive with leaves. A totally different tree. When I had first seen it, from the window of A and O, where I had spent my first two weeks in Lewisburg over a year and a half ago, it was mid-January and the tree was bare of leaves, its thick black limbs stretched high in the sky, the myriad fine branches, like so many imploring fingers, outstretched and empty.

There were no prisoners in the yard. It must be after four, I thought. We arrived at the entrance of the segregation unit, the three-story wing of the main building. The cars stopped. I stashed my pipe tool. We all got out. No one around but us. For a fleeting, absurd moment the idea of running away crossed my mind. Crazy! Nowhere to run. Backward or forward, it's all the same. Can't walk out of here. I followed the others down the stairs into the basement of the building. Inside, in the dimly lit antechamber, we formed a loose circle in what I sensed was an instinctive move. The hacks ordered us to form a single line and we were led through another room, long and rectangular, and then into the area of the hole. We saw the long line of cells through the heavy glass windows on the sides of the barred door. It was dark in that cell block.

"Strip it off." I turned and saw it was Mr. Monster who gave the order. We stripped and put our clothes in the laundry baskets.

"Shoes, shorts, get it all off," he said. "If you got any personal belongings, give them to the man at the window." I carried my pipe and pouch over to the window. Jerry was handing over his huge pocket watch attached to a braided rope that he wore as a belt. We were almost giggling. A giddier bunch of escapees would be hard to find.

"You want this card?" the hack asked David.

"No, it's not mine anyway," David said, laughing.

"Okay. Line up," said Mr. Monster. And we did. Laughing in our nakedness. "Lift your arms. Open your mouth. Run your hands through your hair. Lift your balls. Okay. Turn around. Spread those cheeks. Lift your feet." Each of us went through the ritual; we were not humiliated by this Humiliation Ceremony. The strange movements seemed a prelude to some dance.

The Hole / 76

Dickey "the Worm" continued to wriggle after his turn. David stood on his toes; his legs were together; his arms pressed close to his body; his hands clapped silently. A crazy grin was on his face. The cement floor was cold and we were chilled and tingling from both it and the excitement.

"Okay," the hack said. "On the bench there you'll find shorts, a T-shirt, towel, soap, and a cup. Blankets, too. Pick up your blues at the window. Those slides under the bench are yours, too. Hurry up."

And we got into our new old outfits; the shorts and shirts were clean but ragged and shapeless. The blue pants were clean too, but in shabby condition. I had to roll the cuffs up two or three times. The "slides" consisted of a piece of carpet material the shape of a troll's foot with a crosspiece; slip a foot in one and a man could slide forward but try to walk and the damn thing would slip off the foot as it rose. We stood admiring each other's costumes. We looked like castaways on some desert island. Beachcombers.

"I shall wear my trousers rolled and walk upon the beach," John intoned.

"Okay. Pick up your blankets. Line up."

The jaws of justice were open and about to close. The obstructionists caught between the teeth. The men who took to the field were to be thrown into the pit. Their gentle faces would no longer be seen. What strange food, indeed. Perhaps, with a little luck, we could cause indigestion of the penal system. I picked up my blanket and slid over in front of the hack. David was behind me and the others followed. The door opened and we were led in. The hack stopped before a cell.

"Cook, in here," he said. And I stepped over the lip of the cell, my slides falling off, and the iron door closed loudly behind me. I heard the names of my friends called out, doors opening and closing. Then the steps of the hack returning to the main door. That door slammed shut. It was over. At last, the movement of the day ceased. I was alone. We were all alone, together. This is the "hole."

Standing inside my cell, conscious of the damp floor, and still holding my blankets and sheets in both arms, I turned, silence within and without, to face the door and see what I could see out of the small grated window. No luck. A heavy iron plate covered it from the outside. By squinting through the crack between the plate and the door I could see how the plates were fastened on all the windows of the cells across the corridor. Hinged at the bottom of the window, with a catch at the top, they permitted a hack or an official a protected view of the man inside, while effectively cutting the inmate off from any communication with the other prisoners in the block.

We have disappeared, I thought. Our faces can no longer be seen. Nor can I see anyone's face. Truly, this is to be alone. No great matter. "You have come to terms with loneliness." I heard her voice come out of my past. A poetess. Long black hair, the movements of a sly serpent: clinging yet natural, earthy. We were never able to fill each other's loneliness; our imaginations had already done that for us.

Perhaps all that preparation was but a prelude to this scene, I thought. Certainly, then, I am prepared. Let's make a home of this place. I put my blankets and sheets down on the green, plastic-covered mattress that was on the floor in a corner. I was aware that my feet were not only cold but sticking in places to the floor. Filthy cell. I tried the slides again; by twisting the crosspieces I was able to make them fit tighter around the arch of my foot. Walking became easier. There was little room to walk, however, for the cell was only six feet by nine feet. The damp floor, I realized, was below the ground; that thick window must then be at ground level. I could see the outline of bars beyond the painted glass. I moved the mattress into the middle of the cell, arranged the blankets and sheets in a pile. There was a paper cup with a wash cloth stuck in it. But where's the water? No sink in this cell. I noticed above the shitter, a recess formed by a curved piece of metal with a half-inch nozzle extending from the top. My own private stream. Not flowing now, though. The toilet beneath the recess was a huge square piece of rotting cement work, the bowl cracked and filthy, the seat area resembling some old cement sidewalk damaged by weather and wear. I looked but could find no way to flush it. Sewer bugs and small flies were busy around the bowl. I later realized that the sticky sensation my feet experienced was due to the squashed bugs on the floor. I did not like that toilet at all and dreaded the need to use it; no toilet paper anyway, nor any need beyond a piss. And pissing in unaccustomed solitude was a great relief—until the salty odor rose and filled the cell. Ingenious, I thought; this punishment is designed to make one sick of oneself.

There are enough selves in me to keep me occupied for quite a while, I said to myself. I'll let each one have its day, entertain me, distract me, bore me; then, sick of it, I'll go on to another. Perhaps, at the end of this adventure, there will be no selves to be sick about. There will be no sickness. No punishment, then.

I was pacing around the cell. The green mattress with its pile of blankets and sheets took on the form of an island, a snow-capped mountain at one end. I was growing accustomed to the cell. The walls were becoming familiar; the door was rich in scratches I put off examining. I noticed, too, that as I approached the window from different angles, words took form on the paint. Save all that, too, I thought. It is enough for now to familiarize myself with this cell. It looks like I'll be here for a while. And I walked around and around that island. When I became aware of a dizzy sensation, after too many turns in one direction, I changed course, and tempted vertigo on the other side.

I was pleased that we had arrived, finally, in the cells. All my anxiety about violence at the rear gate and the "latent" cop was gone. We had flowed without interruption into the "hole." Now here, we must not be overcome by it.

How, I asked myself, could I be overcome by this solitude, this simplicity? For over a year I have not had such solitude. The wide spaces of Allenwood never permitted it; the cube really made me more conscious of the slightest noise; one involuntarily became an eavesdropper. But here? Nothing, no one. No world out there to see. Renounce it, then. No relationships to keep up. Forgo them, then. No tensions, no vibrations to be constantly aware of. Forget them, then.

Such simplicity. Shorts, a pair of pants without all the buttons, a T-shirt. No others. Therefore, no vanity. Two blankets, two sheets. I need but one of each. Really, don't need them now.

The Hole / 79

A cup, but no water. So, no desire. A washcloth. Unneeded luxury. A shitter should I need. A room to be alone in; a door to keep danger out, me within. It will do. It will do. Had I my pipe, a book—I could do a good bit in here.

Heavy clanking sounds suddenly invaded the silence; wheels and the rumbling sound of what must be a cart could be heard, then footsteps of guards and low mumbling sounds. The plate in front of my window opened and then disappeared.

"Chow," said the face at the window. He unlocked the door and from the cart the hack took a paper plate filled with food and a paper cup filled with coffee and handed them to me.

"Thanks," I said. There was no reply. Not much ceremony in the "hole." The door slammed shut. I took my meal back to my island and squatted on the peaks of the mountain. Not much food either, I decided. But I was hungry enough to eat the plate, so I didn't mind the thin slab of meat loaf, small scoop of mashed potatoes, string beans (count them), taste of salad, and what might have been pudding. I ate the hunk of bread, too, although I knew I should have saved it for later. I licked the plate clean because the wooden fork just refused to handle the scraps. Not bad, I thought. Quick service, too. I shoved the empty plate across the floor to the door with my foot. I sat and sipped my coffee. The taste of a heated plastic cup.

The hacks, having served the other cells beyond mine and on the other side, were returning to my door.

"Want a flush?" the face said as it suddenly appeared at the open window. I realized then that the window had been left open. I had missed a chance to look around the block.

"Yes," I said. "How about some water?"

"Up your cup there," he said. Simultaneously, the roaring of the toilet beneath and the noisy fast-flowing water from the nozzle into my cup caught me unprepared for such complexity and I stood dazed before it.

"Hey, I'm getting wet," I shouted out the window, as the water from the overflowing cup spilled on the floor.

"Shoulda told me to stop when," he said in a voice I suddenly remembered from my childhood. He's Pennsylvania Dutch, I said to myself.

"Here's some paper," he said. Again, that thick guttural sound that I had not heard for years was speaking to me. And through the grates of the window he stuck a thin roll of toilet paper, all of five segments.

"Thanks," I said, as I stepped in a puddle to get it. The iron plate rose to slam on my face.

Sunset in the "hole" on Sunday evening. Mild and meek it was, too. Not the panoramic, technicolor sunset over Allenwood's lethargic mountain; no thousand shades of red, no thousand colors of blue. Meek it found me, too; but not so mild, after the tensions of that crazy moment—water churning into and out of my cell, the puddle, and the Dutchman. From my below ground level cell, through the yellow, opaque, stationary window, the lower casing parallel with my shoulders, I could not see the sun at all. The small chips in the paint permitted my squinting eye sight of the high brick wall, a road and a tennis court away, and a water tower beyond the wall. But the setting sun shed its last rays, diffused by the mellow-yellow paint, along with the enlarged shadows of the bars beyond the window glass, all over the walls and ceiling. From the earlier, dreary, grime- and filth-encrusted pit, with its bad vibrations, my cell was transformed into a warm, inviting, harmonious space, as patterns of golden yellows and rich browns moved slowly across the cell until the light faded completely.

I walked, calm and thoughtless, throughout that sunset as it came in my window and bathed the green island, streaked across the mountain, and colored my entire world. I had no desire to beat upon the door, as I felt perhaps I was expected to do; nor did this calmness within crave song, "Yankee Doodle," and drum. Nor was I disappointed when the last movement of light and shadow passed. I enjoyed the show.

I heard some sounds coming from the corridor. I put my ear to the crack at the window.

"HEYY, HOBBHOBBITTTTHOBBITT!" I thought I heard the sound of my name, but it was distorted into echo as it traveled down the small iron-walled corridor.

"Is that you, David?" I said, but I could not recognize the

The Hole / 81

sound of my own voice. I tried again.

"Isthat   youDavid?" I said slowly.

"Yes   It'sme," he said, and he sounded happy.

"Whatareyou   sohappyabout?" I asked.

"Thesunset   Hobbit!   Didyousee   it?"

"Yes   Iwalkedthroughit," I said.

"Hey   whereisJerry?" asked John Bach. His voice sounded quite close to me.

"I'mdownhere   nexttoDavid," Jerry said.

"Where'sDickey?" I asked.

"He'sacross   fromme," I heard David's voice say.

"What'reyoudoing?" I asked. And the corridor filled with voices and echoes, driving my head away from the crack.

"I'mdoing   yoga," I heard John's voice say after a long pause as the echoes faded.

"Iwasstanding   onmyhead," David said. "You   shouldtry it   Hobbit."

"Iwasdoing   push-ups   " said Jerry. "Man   doI stink!"

But it was too much of a hassle to keep up the rap under those conditions, and, having made connections and shared the feelings within us, we settled back into the solitude of our cells.

The sound of their voices after long silence refreshed me. They sounded all together, unharried. Yet, in the now dull cell, I was aware of a creeping anxiety within me. We had, indeed, made the walk. Not as I had planned—not with Tom and Mike, anyway; but with young C.O.'s as I had at first hoped. But now here in the hole, none of us was jailwise. In here, we were all innocents. What have I done? I asked myself. Who could tell us what to expect next? The episode of Mrs. Eaton's move still disturbed me; I did not know enough now, any more than I did then, of what was going on. I wondered how she and Bob had made out. I wondered, too, if the crowd or anyone in it had seen us. They didn't appear to be aware of what was happening. If they didn't see us, what a drag. How is it political? I heard Dan say. But then we did not go out of our way to yell, shout, or wave our arms either. At least I didn't. Davy did, though. I thought I remembered delighting in the sight of him jumping up and down; but everything seemed to be happening at once:

hacks approaching from both directions, the sun on my neck, the presence of the crowd, John determined to move on, Jerry tackled. It all came back. Crowded into my cell. I sat down, as if to give all the people room. The agitation in my mind faded away. That crazy glee took its place.

It is a good thing, I thought, that I'm alone. That no one can see this crazy man's face. And I got up and swerved as if to avoid one of my guests. "Is that you, Mr. Rauch?" I heard my own startled laughter echoing in my cell. It was love. That was what it was all about. That's what I heard in David's voice, in Jerry's shouts as we crossed the field. It was still in their voices just now. A crazy love for the whole mess of people around us. That myriad-headed crowd, Mr. Stretch and Mr. Monster. That's what kept his head bobbing back and forth, his eyes seeking my crotch. He had caught the vibrations. But he translated them into his own language. A year and a half in jail has made you lovesick, you crazy Hobbit, I told myself. What mass wooing you've been up to! I suddenly realized, with a twinge of the guilt of my first teenage seduction, what this whole week was all about. That's why there was no anger as that door closed. That's why I was upset with the Dutchman, who spoke out of my youth in Palmerton but caused chaos in my cell. Why didn't he realize it? That's why, for the life of me, I can hate no one. Not Johnson, not Nixon, not Engle. That poor, sad, hung up little man. And Rauch, so super-righteous. And Stretch, beautiful Stretch, and Mr. Stoned: our guardian angels at the rear gate. Too much. "Come in, Mr. Monster. Yes, it's all right. But make your hands behave. Welcome." There ought to be a law against such love. I laughed again. This time I just let it out and the sound danced around my head.

"My wife will file for a divorce when she hears," I told myself. "I hear you've been making love to hundreds of people while you were in jail," I heard her say. "No divorce. Sorry," I said. "Anarchist's marriage, remember? Bless your sweet blond independence."

Move over now, Sweet Babe, and let that red and white cow in. A little pasture, too. How great you are, Mother Earth, to make their platter their bed also. The sun was here a little while ago. The stars will have to do now.

And the crowd. Bring them in, sit them down. It's not a face-less crowd. I know some who were there. Richard and Mary Drinnon, my friends from Bucknell, out of their elegant, one-room schoolhouse home. Remember, Dick, we crawled under-neath it and carried squirrel shit out in buckets before the architects went to work on it. Such times. Such people. We were on our way to you, Dick and Mary. And Joe Rogers, the gentle Quaker, who visits all of us at Allenwood and Lewisburg each month. He was there. Professor Casmir, the laconic Texan, who carried Tolkien's world and Camus into the prison at Allen-wood on Wednesday evenings for a book discussion group meet-ing. He was there. Bring him in. And those students of Bucknell and Lycoming Junior College who came with the professors, said little, stared at us. Bring them in. This is what it is all about. Don't you see? How do lakes fill up, anyway?

Wandering thus in the wide wastes of my mind, I became gradually aware that someone was staring at me. Unheard, the hack had opened the plate in my door and was eyeing me steadily. I wondered if he could see this cell full of people; I decided not to risk telling him of it; I knew about the psycho ward above us on the second floor of this segregation unit; it, too, had cells and not padded ones. The hack, having accom-plished his purpose—I was aware of him now—suddenly dis-appeared. He left the plate down. Great, I thought. And I scrambled off my mountain and rushed to the window to see or hear him opening all the plates, make his count, and leave the block, just as the faces of John and Dickey, diced by the grates in their windows, appeared across from me.

"Hi, John," I said. "How are you?" There was no echo now.

"Great," he said and the word came softly up from inside him.

"Doing yoga?" I asked.

"Yes," he said. "The mattress is excellent for it." And with that his arms, long and graceful, rose like flames above his head and then descended slowly in front of him, taking with them his head and shoulders, finally to disappear from the window. I knew that his hands, now out of sight, wrapped around his ankles; his head was hidden by unbending knees; his long frame was folded, sealed, stamped, and delivered without a word uttered.

"Hey, Dickey! How are you?" I asked.

"I'm great, Jack," he said. "I've been flashing all night. Wow! Hey, Davy, what'cha doing?" he asked. David and Jerry were on the same side of the block as I and were out of my line of vision.

"Looks like they're going to leave these windows open," said David.

"Hey, it must be around eleven o'clock," Jerry said. "The hack was taking a count."

"Hey, Davy," asked John as he reappeared at his window. "Do you have a sink in your cell?"

"Yeah, John, real hot water, too," David said.

"What kind of nonsense is that?" I asked. "I haven't got a sink. Do you, John?"

"No, I've just got a toilet. No flush either."

"Same here," I said. "What else you guys got, anyway? Why all that luxury?"

"That's all, Hobbit, besides the bunk," said David.

"Bunk?" I asked. "John, he has a bunk in his cell."

"A real four-legged bunk?" John asked.

"No, no legs," said David. "It's attached to the wall."

"We must be in strip cells," John said.

"Yeah," I said, and the memory of my crowded cell coupled with the word "strip" and I laughed out loud at the folly of this punishment; soaring now on my long evening's rap with crowds, hacks, and friends, glee bubbling up within me, I shouted out the window.

"Hey, let's have some music! Let's sing!"

Silence. Not a word. I was about to say it again, but I noticed John and Dickey had disappeared from their windows. I felt uneasy, suddenly alone. Inside my cell there was no crowd; there were no faces beaming in corners. Just a spotted mattress with a tangle of blankets and sheets at one end, some squirming bugs on the edge of the plate at my foot, the stench of piss from the toilet—my hand where it pressed against the doorjamb, was dirty.

The Hole / 85

I paced the cell. The silence was awkward. Then I heard repeated flushing of toilets and a churning sound that must be the taps in the sinks. Anxiety raced within me. But time slowed down. As when a gust in a snowstorm whirls past, one can almost see the layer upon layer of blown snow drop slowly to form drifts; so my time—this minute it takes to pace three times around this cell—seemed to fall so slowly, while emotion raced on in front of me, overtook me from behind: lack of confidence piled on top of feeling abused. My mountain had become a valley; where many were I was now alone; doubts piled on doubts. I stubbed my toe on the base of the toilet.

"Hey, Dickey," I heard John say, "how about a game of chess?"

"Dig it," said Dickey. "Wait till I get ready. There's a scrap of paper under my mattress."

The tension was broken. We all listened to the chatter of the chess game in preparation. I stood quietly at the door. The light in the corridor had been turned off, but inside each occupied cell the light, caged in a small barred box above the door, was kept on. It would be on all night, all day.

"Hey, Dickey, you can't play chess!" yelled David. "You can't even play checkers."

"Yeah, Dickey, what's the idea of conning us along with this crap?" Jerry broke in. "We know you can't play chess."

"Tell 'em, Jack," Dickey said to me. "Tell 'em how I was playing in the reading room with Bill Curry. Tell 'em."

"He was," I said. "I saw it. I'm telling you it's true. Weirdest fucking game I ever saw in my life. He wore Billy down by constant attrition. Getting up, leaving, coming back, rocking, getting up. Drove Billy insane."

I could see through John's grate, directly across from me, the yellow window of his cell, a darker yellow now against the night. John was walking around his cell. He would appear, then disappear. He did not have to prepare for the game; he could play it in his head. Dickey kept up his constant chatter about how he had just learned the game and was asking John about where the queen should be placed, how certain moves were made. Under his light, Dickey was bobbing up and down as he made his men on the floor and came up to ask a question or get an answer from John, his shadow barely having time to come together on his wall.

I had taken the wrong tack. I had tried to shove my enthusiasm, my cell full of folk, down their throats. We are all fire-eaters, but not all necessarily at the same time. If I craved song so much, I should have sung myself, not try to create it in them. All I did was spoil things. Exhibiting my high when they were not high. Too much of that and real chaos can set in. That awkward silence, embarrassing standstill. John was right in suggesting chess. Let me go by, sink in my cell, think it over. We all have to do the silent bits in our own way. The game is good; it distracts while taking up time. I cannot play that game, but it delights me to hear Dickey play it.

I relaxed. The emotional load I had been carrying seemed lighter. We all had such loads, I realized, haphazardly distributed in each of us. Alone each of us might go under, panic perhaps; but if we threw it all together into the middle—somewhere in this corridor—we could make it. All five of us could carry it then.

I picked up the paper cup of water from the toilet's wide cement rim. But in doing so I saw the inside of that filthy bowl, its stains, bugs, and crud, and realized that this water I was about to drink had been close to that filth for hours. It rested on filth, too. I could not drink it. I stood there holding the cup. I wanted to set it somewhere. But the only raised surface in the cell was that damned shitter. I went over to the window. There was no ledge. The casing of the window met the cement wall without interruption, except where a former inmate had dug under the casing to make a little ledge that might hold a pencil. It didn't. Where was I to put this water that I would not drink? I couldn't throw it away. Couldn't pour it into that scummy pool. It was still clean. In this cup it moved from side to side, lapping at the edges like the waves against Staten Island Ferry. Weird notion, that, I thought: water within a cup, splashing at the sides, resembles water breaking against the sides of a ferry. Where is that idea taking me? I said to myself. And I thirsted for that water. I was on fire inside: the conflagration of all that day's accumulated experiences and emotions, the joy and the anxiety, that leap over the fence and the crotch-happy cop, my crowded cell followed by that humiliating emptiness. It was all burning inside and I had no water to drink. This little lake, alive and churning as I walk, will not be disturbed by me. Where to put it? Goddamn this infernal institution that does not provide for a cup of plain water! That does not provide for me and this thirst! For I'll not put out this fire with this water. Nor will I throw it away. We are alone in this cell. We have shared the filth of a common toilet. I'll not make an end of it. Let it be. It seems to like it where it is. It even sparkles. I did not desire it anymore. I was glad to have it with me in this cell. I have water, at least. My own little lake, sparkling.

John must have a lake. Dickey, David, and Jerry, too. How many others have lakes in their cells in this building, I wonder? If all of us on all floors emptied all our lakes and reservoirs into the corridors, we might have a flood that would carry this bloody institution away. But that is just why they don't give inmates in strip cells sinks or regular toilets or toilet paper in rolls. So they can't fuck up the plumbing. But it's the plumbing of this damned institution that should be fucked up! Let it back up on itself and go down in the filth of its own system!

This little cup holds the secret (and I looked askance at my own raving). It is all together in there. Gentle, looked at from here. But in itself, and if augmented in the right proportions, it can be firm. So firm it could clean out these stables, undermine the foundations, wash away the officials and all their phony crap about rehabilitation and justice.

If only we could combine our thirst, our rage, our fire, with that gentleness, firmness, and simplicity. Then when the time came to spill ourselves upon the institutions that confine, the governments that oppress, what a revolution would take place? We would all know the way, for it would be lit by our fires, our rage. We would be carried on by a joy all people possess, the awareness of being simply what they are. We would be carried along in common by streams flowing into one massive churning force, that would not merely wash this brutal anachronism away, but introduce such change that even our own hung up selves would be altered by such a free-flowing coming together, such a joint effort at picking up each other's burdens, the weight of our accumulated misfortunes, the heavy load of the human condition confined.

Chained, we can change. Changed, we can unchain.

I sat down cross-legged on my island. The mountain rose at the other end. The cup of water was in my hands. I was terribly awake. My senses were sharp and clear. The light from the caged bulb above the door reflected off the window behind me and shed a yellow glow on my hands. I was ready. Had I a fire I could cook with this cup, I thought. Silly, Hobbit. A paper cup would burn. No cooking. Nothing to cook, anyway. Guests have gone, too. Offering, I said to myself, I can offer it. Well, do that then if you're so foolish as not to drink it when you're so thirsty. I will offer it together with this little bug I just noticed floating in it. He sacrificed himself just now. No, he's still alive. He's just in for a swim. No stagnating elements in our offering. Nourishment and play. How's that for a ceremony? That bug isn't going to nourish very many. Where's the food? In the water. We've been through that. Not something floating in the water, but the water in the water, the whatness in the isness, the being-in-the-being. Damned scholastic. How those monks messed with your head. Where are you going to take it to offer it? Can't move cross-legged like that. Yes, that's a difficulty that only time can alter. The place is unfortunately confining, my foolish meditations I can't even write down, my position lacks responsibility. But I can sit here with this water that is real and protect it. Not let it be spilled wastefully, used thoughtlessly. I will just sit here and offer it silently. I will sit here and be colored by the light and that window.

"Hey, Hobbit," I heard David call. "You still awake?"

"Yes, I'm all awake," I said from my seat.

"Good night, Hobbit," he said. "Good night, John, Dickey, Jerry. I'm tired. Sleepy time comes."

"Good night, Davy," and all our voices joined him, stretched out, his hands behind his head, grinning wildly at the stars, as we had seen him so many times before, on the green field between the dorms or in his bunk in The Jungle.

The Hole / 89

The walls of Warden Parker's prison split apart. There was no stopping it. When such walls attempt to confine such goodness, then that evil is bound to spend itself, to destroy itself, to have its strength turned upon itself. Nothing, certainly not those walls, could keep the five of us apart.

"Breakfast," said the hack at the window. His face disappeared. I struggled into consciousness. The door opened.

"Hand me that plate," he said, the tone of his command changing in midstream from gruffness to almost a gentleness. I must have appeared exceedingly vulnerable, half-awake as I was and unthinkingly obedient to his order.

"Here you go," he said as he took the empty plate with one hand and gave me a full one with the other. Then coffee.

"I'll be back for your flush and water," he said as he put the plate up in front of the window. Still not together, I just nodded.

There was an orange, a real orange on that plate in my hand. A large, round Sunkist Florida Orange. I could hardly believe it. I sat down to look at it. All the other stuff on the plate was all too familiar: oatmeal, the color and texture of that cement————. No, let's not think about that now. Look at the orange.

"Hey   didyouguys   getan orange?" I heard Jerry yell.

"Yeah," cried Dickey. "It'sneat. Howdidyou   sleep?" he asked Jerry.

"Likeababy," Jerry said. "Areyouup,   Davy?" he asked.

"Uh   ugh." He was up. "HEYYY," he suddenly shouted. "DOODOYOUHAVE! DOOYOUHAVEANANORORANANGEE?"

"Goback   tosleep   Davy," Jerry said after the echo faded and silence once more came into the cells to meet the morning as it came through the window.

Around midmorning the main door of the block opened and I expected it to be lunchtime; but instead we heard Bob Eaton and Alex Futterman greet us each by name and cause us all to strain at the cracks in our doors for a glimpse of their passing. The corridor resounded to our glee and merriment. I was shocked at first, and I wondered why they had been punished. What did they do? Then it was clear to me: they had chosen to flow in behind us, join us. It was too much. They were full of news; we were full of questions.

"Wethought wejustcouldn't letyouguys stayhereallby yourselves," explained Eaton. "So we wentupto theofficeand toldthem wewererefusingto work."

"Yeah, wethoughtyou mightneed somecompany," Alex said.

"Youmissed thebestpart," said Eaton. "Theguyswentwild Theywereallin theparkinglot Tonycussed outRauch tohisface 'Youdirtymotherfuckingsonofabitch!' Tonycalled him whenyouguys wereputintothecars Helostsome gooddaysoverit."

"Hey Jack" Alex shouted. "I'vegot amessagefrom Tony foryou."

"What isit?" I asked.

"Hesays totellyou you'reneat," Alex said.

"Is thatit?" I asked.

"That'sit," he said.

"Whathappenedto Bill Boss?" David asked.

"Hestoppedat thefence," Eaton said. "Hecouldn't take hisguitar into the field,hesaid."

"He'sreallytaking alotof ribbingfromtheguys," Alex said. "EspeciallyTommy yourfriendJack Heandtheotheryoung Italians arereallyputtinghim down."

"Yeah," said Eaton. "He'snot toohappyright now."

"Whataboutall myjunk?" Jerry asked.

"Oh letmetellyou Afteryouguys weredrivenoff the guysallgottogether andwentaroundtoeachplace andgot yourstuff out Jack Tomtookcare ofyourpipes and Billy'sgot mostofyourgoodbooks Somestuff heleft."

"Wegotthebox oflettersDavid fromunderyourbunk," Alex said. "Westashed allyourcontraband Davy."

"Theydidn't waitlongtobegin gettingyourstuff outof yourcube Jack," Eatonsaid. "Hackswere intherethismorning Yourhomeisgone tooJerry."

"Can'tkickme intoJungle," David said. "I'malreadythere."

"Hey," said Eaton. "Wegottheflag lastnight!"

"Theflag," John said.

"Yeah, Beach,Kelly,Tony,andI Samwatchedout forus

Theyleftit up forsomereason Soafterthenineo'clockcount wescopedit anditlookedgood Samgaveme thego aheadsign butthehackwasstanding inthedoorway Samis somethingelse Thehackdidn'tseeus though Tony'skeeping-it outatthefarm He'sgonna getitoutlater."

"Telluswhathappened withyourmother,Bob," I asked. "What wasthat allaboutanyway?"

"Didyouhear thecrowdinhere?" Eaton asked.

"Whatcrowd?" I asked.

"Thedemonstrators TheyleftAllenwood andcamehere Wefoundout lastnight Five people at first Thenmore thanahundred fromWorkReleaseguys RightuptotheWall shoutingFreedom Guyswereansweringthemtoo."

"Ididn'thear anycrowd," Dickey said. "DidyouJohn?"

"Couldn'thearit fromhere," John said.

"Didyourmother tellthemwewerehere? Aboutthewalk? orwhat?" I asked impatiently. I needed to know what had happened. The tensions were getting higher. It was a drag to have to communicate this way. I didn't hear everything that was being shouted. I could not think and stare at nothing through that crack in the door . . . The strain was too much. I turned away. Make house, I said to myself. Wait, let's eat the orange.

And I peeled my orange slowly, careful not to drop any of the skin. I had plans for the skin. I put the peeled orange and the skin on the plate near the door of the cell. Then I folded the blankets and folded the sheets. The mountain rose and was soon snow-capped again. I put two pieces of orange peel in my cup of water and placed it on top of the mountain. Orange water, I said to myself. If I concentrate maybe I can believe it is tea with oranges. The sweet smell of orange rose from the cup. How about that! Didn't have that at Allenwood. The sun was gentle in the cell.

Thunder in the cell. Thunder in the corridor. The main door was unlocked, the grating sound of metal on metal, the rolling screech of that cart, the loud voices of hacks shouting to each other—it all came in with a shock. It's just lunchtime, I told my frightened self. Calm down. You almost knocked the cup over. What would Kierkegaard think of you—in fear and trembling

The Hole / 92

over the sound of lunch. Nonsense. Let their empty sounds roll. They won't catch me unaware again. Can't let lunch upset me.

Thus I sought to calm myself. But the sounds and noises seemed to go on and on. No end to them. All through lunch iron plates opened, closed, doors slammed shut, again the plates, "Yes, a flush," again the slam. Finally, the main door crashed on the retreating hacks and their annoying service cart.

Alex was telling John, his best friend at Allenwood, that he had wanted to go on the walk. John knew that. But his visit came. He had to see his visit. The rapping went on. I still had my orange.

It lasted a long time. I savored each segment for ten runs around my cell. It was good while it lasted. But my mind was uneasy despite the taste of orange in my mouth: so inappropriate to the conditions of this body, this mind. Daybreak in my mouth, I thought. Storm and trembling everywhere else. I hoped the other guys were not going through this business. It wouldn't be good now to talk about it.

My mind was anxious in its ignorance of what had happened. How did the crowd come to be at this wall? Did they see us at all? Is that why? What happened to Bob's mother? Where was he during all of it?

I tried to reach Eaton again when a pause in the echoing rap provided a space. From him I heard, but not clearly nor in sequence, that the crowd had not seen us at all. That he thought it was his friend Candy Putter who made the call for the demonstration to move here. That his mother told the officers she was going to walk off the compound and why she was doing it; that they had a hilarious (to Bob) rap with her about it. That since she hadn't a car and refused to call the taxi that had brought her there, there was little they could do about it; that she was somewhere while we were being driven away (I remembered then the two-way radio announcement mentioning Mrs. Eaton as we sat in the rear of the station wagon). That Bob had tried to walk with his mother but they locked him up in Engle's office instead. That there was some sort of confrontation between Rauch and Mrs. Eaton at the gate in front of newspapermen. That Tony and he had been brought before a hastily convened

The Hole / 93

Adjustment Committee, headed by Engle, and their "good days" for May were being withheld, those three or four days a month the system gives an inmate for adjusting well to a minimum security prison.

Thunder again. Our rap was drowned out by the clanking of doors and heavy tread of hacks. Cells were opened and cursing, defensive men were ordered inside, and, from the tension in the voices and the shuffling, it seemed as if they were being pushed or thrown into the cells.

I retreated again. Agitated in mind and feeling a weakness in my legs, I squatted down away from the blankets and sheets.

None of what Bob said, or what I thought I heard him say, was clear, and much of it was disappointing. I was upset that the crowd did not know of the walk. My pride was affronted. And Mrs. Eaton's ploy seemed confusing. I thought she had been ready to walk. That's why we waited. That's why he left when we did. Why did she have to tell them all about it? What could she tell them, anyway? What did she know about it? Some interpretation, I thought. Translated into Quakerese. That extra mile. What explanation did Engle or Rauch need? We were walking out of their bloody prison! That was explanation enough for jailers. And how did Bob know about the gate confrontation if he was locked up in Engle's office? It sounded too much like a bit of upstaging. Another victory for the publicity conscious. I was angry. What kind of silly-ass effect would that kind of action have on a crowd of antiprison demonstrators? The old file-in-the-cake updated. Mama walks out of prison with her son. Good copy.

I knew my anger and agitation had been evident in my questions to Bob. That did not help the tensions any. They were probably angry with me. But it seemed clear to me, and it must be clear to the others, that our walk went unnoticed by the demonstrators. That meant all that movement, all that anxiety had been without any effect on the crowd. That they did not come here to this wall because of us. That other things—and what things, I thought—had occupied the newspapermen and officials. I struggled with Insignificance and Futility.

So what are we doing in these cells? Why are we guests of

The Hole / 94

Warden Parker, anyway? I got up and began to pace the cell. I was growing more and more agitated. But, at the same time, I was conscious of that cup of water on top of the sheets and blankets. It seemed so calm, so untroubled. My pacing did not disturb it. I decided to change the orange peels. Let's have some freshness in here, I told myself. We're here. Might as well make the best of it.

There was nothing to do but accept it all. Sounds like it went over well in camp, anyway. Some good in it. I thought about Bill Boss getting the business from Sam and his friends. I would hate to get it from them. They're pros. Poor Bill. Beautiful Tony came into my mind. Cussed out Rauch. Damn. That's more than I did when I saw him there. Good for you, Tony! I wished that he was there with us. We'd be all together then. But this is a good group. Seven of us now. Who knows? Maybe tomorrow we'll have more. Both Eaton and Alex would have been with us but for visits. It is good this way. Everyone's here because they want to be. No force used. Not even intimidation caused it all. It happened all so suddenly. Mrs. Eaton and the chaos cut out those who were uncertain. And those of us who were ready beforehand ended up doing it spontaneously. That's the way it should be done. Must be done if it's to work. Voluntarily coming together. No leaders. What the hell, I told myself, I almost didn't go on it after Mrs. Eaton arrived. I needed time to think about it all. Glad I didn't think too much.

I sat down across from the mountain and stared at the cup of water and the floating pieces of orange peel.

That night I took David's advice and tried to stand on my head. It didn't work. I fell over on my backside repeatedly. I cheated a little and moved the mattress up against the wall. Then with my toes touching the wall above, my arms cradling my head below, I made it for a while. But I felt absurd: as if my head were an egg and all my body's weight its brooding hen. After that, I watched in envy John's graceful movements as he went through his exercises. There was less chatter this night; we were too conscious of the silent men who had been put into cells near us. We did not know them. Eaton and Dickey played chess. Futterman rapped with John, and I listened to the spontaneous rap of David and Jerry, who were not conscious of the warmth they generated, the good vibrations their innocent banter created.

Eaton suggested that he write to one of his lawyers, a Jewish friend of his, who was interested in filing a class suit against the Federal Prison System on behalf of all prisoners who are confined in segregation units. It would mean meetings with his lawyer, making appeals against conditions in the "hole," and the protracted involvement of courts and suits.

The anarchist in me rebelled from such a ticky-tacky use of judicial procedure; I disliked playing their game according to their rules in their sandlot. I could not believe that in their strange minds our jailers had any more respect for the law than I did. To try to influence them in this legal fashion served really to bolster appearance, rather than to strike at the core of them. We didn't reach Mr. Stretch and Mr. Stoned through lawsuits.

But if it could possibly help some inmates, I could not really defend such an absolute position. I thought of the defensive tones that curbed the anger of those men who were shoved into the cells nearby; they had not said a word all night as we rapped on as if oblivious to this environment. Besides, we are more or less articulate; we have words to give to things. Perhaps such articulation, the efforts of all seven of us, could do a little toward changing some of the more gross deficiencies in here. No sink, no water to drink, no tooth powder. Nothing to read, no flush on the toilet. No air. I was increasingly aware, especially after my afternoon exercises—push-ups, sit-ups, running-in-place, and some isometric exercises within the doorway—that I smelled. In-fucking-deed, I stank.

A lawsuit might be useful to other prisoners. I couldn't ask them to share my weird politics before I made any effort to help them, even granting I could help them.

So I told Eaton that I'd go along with the suit business if all the others wanted it. That generated some lively commotion from David and Jerry. They dug having lawyers they wouldn't have to pay. So it was agreed that Eaton would write his letter the next day and we would all soon be represented by counsel.

The idea amused me. I had never employed a lawyer before. My first lawyer, I told myself. Here I am in a strip cell and I get a lawyer handed to me on a paper plate.

I made it clear to Bob, and told him I would make it clear to his lawyer, that I did not wish to have our little walk defended in any court by any lawyer. That belonged to a different order of things. To attack this prison system through suits might be in harmony with the established order (dissonant as it was) and bring about some long neglected reforms, but I was not interested in pleading not guilty to any of my actions. I had no faith in the judicial system, nor any craving for reform. I wanted this brick building dismantled, not refurnished; torn down, not propped up by good intentions followed by apathetic gestures.

But, I told myself, my power to tear down the walls of this prison was nowhere, whereas our power to annoy wardens, associate wardens, and possibly Washington bureaucrats, was somewhere at least.

Our forefathers are responsible for the existence of this prison, for the system of unhallowed (that is, righteous) concepts upon which it was based and continues, despite the liberal rhetoric of our day, to operate. It is fitting, I thought, that my Quaker friend Bob Eaton should initiate a suit against injustices in the "hole." The "hole" was introduced centuries ago into our penal system by Quakers, intent on giving the wayward enough solitude to convert them to better social behavior.

Let's do it, Bob. But let's do it with a little finesse. That means for me, anyway, to do what we must do, what we feel we have to do; and not to be influenced by what lawyers might think of it or how it would look in court. To make our calls joyous, not prudent in the legal or religious sense. To be bold enough to let actions speak, not mouthpieces prevaricate. To reach for the core of persons, not for the loopholes of laws. To make our words match our deeds, not some judicial formula. In so doing, to delight in the echo awakened in other men. Above all, let us not hope. Let us not waste any energy in putting hope in the court system or in lawyers. I've seen too many inmates die too many times from overdoses of Hope in lawyers on the street, cases in court, Justice in the mouths of judges.

The Hole / 97

It is not an understanding of the law that is needed; what is needed is an understanding of how men think and where their torn-up psyches will take them, and what happened to be going down when, so stirred, they moved into some mistake. What is needed is not law at all—Error gowned and wigged. What is needed is some penetrating understanding, much sharing of responsibility, and more forgiveness than any of us are capable of. "Enough or Too much" as Blake said. Thus armed, our judges would with impunity exceed their own limitations and that of the law as well. In doing so, with certainty they would be doing right. In doing right consistently, they might tempt greatness. But, assuredly, they would inflict less pain, less suffering.

My head hurt. Might as well stand on it, I said to myself, as I lowered to my knees and then sprang up from behind, my toes coming to rest on the wall. I can see clearly a part of this wall I otherwise would have neglected. I wondered if the headstand had thus achieved its purpose. Oh, David, what am I to do now that I'm standing on my head in the "hole"? The core of me has not changed. There I am as dependent on you, on all those whom I love, as ever I was. This stance is stationary. I cannot walk on my hands as Jerry can, my head cannot toss and beat about as Dickey's. But at the root of me I am tossing to and fro. My peaks are but preludes to depressions. The bitter and the sweet stand in line, one after the other, as we stand to get our laundry, meals, visits. I cannot beat the drum as Alex does, nor sing as John does. But the skin of my psyche is beaten on, the walls of me receive strange vibrations. Staring at the cement block is more limiting than these confining walls. How long must we wear these concrete blinders?

Enough. We will wear them until the end. I descended, or rather my legs came down. My head felt cracked. Too much brooding.

I dreamed that I had walked into a room in which a group of heavy, dark-suited men sat around a table. The table was large and round and almost filled the room, which was darkened above and in all the corners. My purpose, it seemed to me, was to go around the men at the table and out the door on the other

The Hole / 98

side of the room. Some of the men were just shadowy forms to me. I could only see their backs as I passed behind them. Others, far off to the right, I could not see at all. One man, sitting not far from the door I was approaching, lifted his head and calmly, almost with disinterest, watched as I moved around the table. His head was large and round and he was balding. When I arrived at the door, I discovered it was blocked by what appeared to be a heavy wooden structure about waist-high. The top of it was as wide as it was deep. It filled the entire space before the door and I knew it would have to be moved. I found I could budge it a little bit at a time and I was confident that I could in time move it away from the door. But as I budged it I became conscious of a huge globe or ball that was on top of the structure as if on a pedestal. I had not seen the globe, if that was what it was, because it was invisible. That realization did not seem too strange to me. Looking at it, I could perceive no substance to it; yet I was vaguely aware at certain places of its outer circular lines. What seemed odd was my predicament. I had to move the pedestal, but if I moved it that weird beach-ball-for-the-blind would fall off. I knew I had to remove it before I could tackle the pedestal. I call it a pedestal because the globe or whatever was resting upon it. The wooden structure seemed devoid of any decoration—no columns, carvings, or inscriptions. Perhaps it was a solid piece of wood. All I knew was that it was heavy. And it blocked my way.

I put my hands and forearms under the globe as if it were a huge cannonball or one of those heavy balls that are used in gyms for losing weight. I found I could not lift it at all. The weight of it must be tremendous, I thought. It was very strange now because I could see my fingers, bloodless and strained, and my forearms and wrists, pressed flat against the globe like a young boy's nose against a candy store window. The veins in my arms were enlarged and quite blue and flat, like highways in a child's coloring book. I could not see this weight that so strained my arms. I could only feel it all the way to the tips of my fingers.

I decided to roll it toward me and cradle it with my body. I thought if I could get my body next to it, I could lower myself and it to the floor. But as the globe approached the edge of the pedestal, I felt its enormous weight on me. And I grew afraid. At the edge, I stayed it. I felt that it would not remain there of itself. I wondered how it remained in the middle. There was nothing else on top of the pedestal. I could not keep it stationary, however, and I cupped my body to receive as much of its bulk as it could and stretched my arms to their limits more around than underneath the globe. But in that instant when the globe all but left the edge, when its weight seemed no longer to have that pedestal but me to rest upon, when my body felt that great pressure, I grew most terrified and with fear pushed up and against that globe. It would have fallen heavily to the floor. It would have gone right through me, plunged down through my gut. I would have been helpless to contain or hinder it. I could not take that risk. It was as I was struggling to return that globe to the center of the pedestal that I woke to face a piercing white ball from the blackness in front of me. I quickly turned my head to the wall.

It's just the hack making his count, I thought. I lay there in the silence. The sound of his steps died away. Just another jail-house dream, I said to myself. They were common. All of us had them. Davy told his yesterday. Jerry, too. Sometimes in such a dream you are outside in some familiar place but anxious and afraid. Sometimes you are escaping with strangers or lovers or with your mother and father. Sometimes, the saddest times, you are coming back and hoping that they have not missed you.

About noontime on the third day, the thundering main door opened again and then my door was opened.

"Come on. We got a new cell for you," the hack said. And I picked up my blankets, sheets, and cup, and stepped over the lip of the cell. He went before me down the corridor and opened the cell next to David. I saw David's name on the yellow card about his door.

"Hey, David," I said. "I'm moving uptown."

"Great, Hobbit," David said. And I took up my new residence. John was then moved out of his strip cell and put in one across from me.

"Hey, John   wemadeit!" I shouted. "Asink   and hotwater

andarealtoilet   Itevenflushes." And both of us played with our new acquisitions.

"Doyou   havesoap?" John asked me.

"Yeah," I said. In the small sink there was a piece of soap the size of those wrapped bars in motels. I recognized it as the kind occasionally distributed at Allenwood. It was bad soap. It seemed diffused already with body odor. But it was soap. I filled the sink with hot water, stripped down, and took a birdbath. The hot water felt good as it splashed over me. I had reached the point where I could hardly stand my own stench, especially my armpits. My hair, long and uncombed, felt greasy and my scalp itched. I just stood there naked in my cell and poured hot water over me from my cup. I didn't care if the floor got wet. Then I soaped down with the washcloth that had gone unused in my former cell. Such wealth, I thought. I looked about my new estate. There was time to examine it, a new window and a door full of graffiti. I could not really decide if I preferred my stench to that of the soap. The rinse was best of all. My body seemed washed as if for the first time. It felt new and I felt strangely alert and eager, I hoped, for the impossible—that the routine that after three days held nothing new for me would change. I filled the cup repeatedly with cold water and stood there naked and drank each cup as if it were beer on an unlimited tab. Give the house a drink, I said to myself.

I could hear John splashing in his cell across from me. Our first bath had not been a silent one. But the guys in the other cells were all silent. I peered out of the crack, but I couldn't see anything. This crack is even smaller than the other, I said to myself.

Later, as I was sitting cross-legged on my mattress eating supper, the hack came by again.

"Got a letter, Cook," he said. "I'll slip it under the door. You want paper and a pencil?" he asked.

"Yes, an envelope, too," I said. I stooped down and caught the corner of an envelope where it curved up at the base of the lip and pulled on it. I did not look at the handwriting. It was enough just to have a letter now in this cell. I backed up to the mattress and put the letter, face down, beside me. Save it for awhile, I said to myself.

"Here's your paper and pencil," I heard the hack say. And I got up and took them, rolled up in an envelope, from the grate where they were stuck.

"Thanks," I said.

At least I didn't have to wait to hear my name called out. What a drag that is. He just said, "Got a letter, Cook." Relatively painless, considering. I finished my meal. In what remained of my toilet paper issue for the day, I wrapped the piece of cake remaining from supper. It would fill the emptiness tonight. I cleaned house. One must prepare for the evenings, I told myself. The floor was dry now. I arranged the mattress and blankets. Somehow, with the convenience of a sink and running water, the image of my island and its snow-capped mountain was more difficult to sustain. I realized then what really prohibited my fancy. On top of the sheets was the letter the hack delivered, along with the sheet of lined seventh grade paper, an envelope, and a pencil. I had a sudden yearning for my old cell with its barren simplicity. This one, although it did not have a bunk, was becoming complicated.

How does one do "mail" in the "hole"? I pondered. At Allenwood it is such a hassle. The four o'clock mail call.

"Come and get your mail! Jones, Smith, O'Malley, Gonzalez, Frank No. 30072 Jones, O'Brien, George Root, Harry Nobody, John Forgotten, Larry Dismissed. Here's one for you at last, Sam. Where's Left Over? Here's your lawyer, Lost John. Someone die, Joe? Why so gloomy? It's from Welfare, Bill. Your wife's okay. Lost parole, Henry. Heard about it at the office. Sloane. McNamara. George. Felix, it's over. No chance, Duke. Mike, you're shafted. Nothing for you, Al. Sorry. It's been a long time. Why don't you write one to yourself. We'll mail it together. The judge is on vacation, Mac. No luck. Here's something from the Warden. Sorry, Associate Warden. You know Parker doesn't read his own mail. What's this? A Christmas card? Who's Sebastian Pax? Some fucking C.O., I bet. It's almost summertime. Where's Harry, it's another bill. Leave Steve alone there, his wife is bound to write one of these days. Clide, your daughter's pregnant. Bill, your mortgage is due and so is the loan. Denied

Halfway House, Pete? Sorry. Bank robbers are not rehabilitative. Your mother loves you, Jerry. Second letter in a week. That school wants your money, Mickey. Tell 'em to go to hell. Your wife wants more money, Tom. What are you going to say this time? Need help? Who got locked up? Why? He just got out of here. What the hell, let it all go down. No, I don't want *Time* magazine. Still no word, Paul? It's been how long? When's that baby due, anyway? Who got you that job? How about fixing me up? Here, Homer, let Howie read it for you. Same as last week, right? Hey, Pepe! The court has not ruled in your favor. He says you got a good chance at parole. Believe it! Man, how long you been down, anyway? Who was violated? How? A traffic ticket? Goddamn their eyes! What did they say? Either a deathbed visit or the funeral? One or the other? And if you don't have enough money for you and the marshal, what happens then? Nothing. The city buries her. What can I say? Lost good days? How many? Only ten? What about parole? Lost it. No chance? Out. Whata ya gonna do? Fuck it. Hey, Al, your son is in jail. Drugs. Got 'em in the Tombs. His wife's on welfare. So the decision applies? So what? You have no more money for lawyers. Didn't he say that in the last letter? Sit tight, Buddy, you got years in front. Who gets this *Peacemaker* thing? Where are the fucking C.O.'s? Such shit. Your *Playboys* are up at the office. No pasting them on lockers. What do you think this is, a fucking bedroom? Your daughter graduated? Congratulations! She was just a little girl last you saw? Sorry, Ed. Soon, soon. The other had a baby? No shit. He's a cop? Too bad. Where's Carl? Where's the newly-wed? If this isn't a Dear John letter, I'll eat it. Your turn this week, Carl baby. Louie last week. Claude the week before. Has he heard about Louie the Lip, Boys? Better tell him. He's gotta be prepared. That's it, Men. No more mail."

Mail call always reminded me of a scene from a movie about medieval England. I saw it so long ago that I had forgotten the name, the plot, everything. Only one scene remained with me. The good guys were about to be captured by the bad guys. They had retreated, and finally in a wide green meadow they halted. At this point it looked so like those scenes in Westerns where Indians surround the circle of wagon trains. The bad guys had them surrounded. The good guys, about fifty or a hundred of them, formed concentric circles around their leader in the middle. They were ready to fight to the end. The bad guys in far greater number, a veritable army, methodically and without haste formed in ranks around the smaller body of men. I was fascinated by the detached way the leader of the bad guys marshaled his men in concentric circles, also, but of vastly greater size. He seemed to have had it all worked out beforehand. I was prepared, after a childhood of Westerns, for the Indian tactic of circling, screaming, galloping warriors, whose effect was more psychological than practical. They made few scores on the inside, for shooting bows on horseback at high speed, I understood, would be difficult. Then the Kamikaze leaps by braves into the circle of settlers, etc. I was not prepared for what transpired on the screen in Merry Old England. And that was probably why it remained with me. Having gathered his forces around the good guys, the bad leader from his comfortable coach gave an order, with a tired gesture of his hand, and from the outer circle of his troops, in beautiful symmetry, there rose with rainbow precision thousands of arrows all destined to fall within that inner circle of good guys. And they did. And no one could do anything abut it. All the weapons of the good guys, all their rage and courage—all of it was useless.

Another tired gesture and another wide circle of arrows arched up, like boys peeing around a puddle, and inevitably the arrows hit some of those in the inner circle, who were quite defenseless themselves and had nowhere to go anyway. Their ranks became less orderly as a result of fallen and injured men. The circle of good guys standing more or less unpunctured became smaller and smaller with each cascade of arrows until finally, the leader having fallen, perhaps only fifteen or twenty of his men remained. They still surrounded him. The end was clearly near. And with an impossibly casual movement of the bad guy's hand, the final onslaught of arrows filled the sky above, from what appeared to be every rank, every circle, from each and every bow, like some myriad-mouthed Roman fountain, and fell and found all the targets remaining. Quite dead that porcupine.

Thus, only slightly exaggerated, is mail call in prison. Incredible. But that is mail call on a large scale. That is to view it as affecting all prisoners—God's-eye view, if you will. What is it to an individual, one inmate? I said to myself, Self, what is the jailbird's eye view of mail call? Glad you asked, my self replied. (This evening will pass, too, I heard still another voice pipe in.)

Let's keep the arrows. Do away with the army on the outside and the support of friends on the inside, and what do we have left? A bloody St. Sebastian, I told myself. That's a little heavy. Anything lighter than Sebastian? Not if you want to keep arrows in your image, there isn't. Dylan and Stephen were stoned. Yes, but arrows come out of the sky in such graceful arcs, at least when great distances have to be covered. And when they hit, they penetrate. Rocks and stones bounce off, after all. Bruises, nothing more. Well, there's William Tell. Absurd. How about Custer? Custer? He got what we deserve. You're messing with my metaphor. As the Indians say to us today, "Custer died for your sins." In all the Westerns I can recall, the good guys either die or don't die from one arrow, which a John Wayne can easily pull out. Instant recovery. And all the Indians die after being shot once. Never much reality to our flicks.

How real then is El Greco's St. Sebastian? You're back to him. He's too heavy, I told you. He's all you got. Well, which St. Sebastian? There are two of El Greco's, you know. His early one: the one where he deliberately distorts his figure for the first time. Well, now, that's true. As I remember, that Sebastian was a colossus of a man: huge arms, muscular chest, straining thighs, but a small head and almost a tiny hand. Yes, but you're evading the point. He has only one arrow stuck in him. In the left side of the belly. Not particularly damaging. No blood at all. And if I recall, there are a couple of arrows in the tree. So it isn't as if we're looking at the first shot.

But that was the early Sebastian. El Greco was not forty years into his time. The Inquisition, Jesuits, constant war, poverty, people and books burned at the stake, only orthodox art permitted. His later Sebastian. How about that?

Agreed. More arrows, less tree, blood. An oval canvas. No

The Hole / 105

landscape at all. No land, you mean. Just the blazing flame of Sebastian. And a small part of the tree trunk above his head with sky and cloud on either side of him. Yes, dark stormy sky on his right; mild summer sky on his left. Yes, it's all coming back. There is no mountain, no small figures off in the distance, no leaves, no massive stone to kneel upon, no straining to get away. Funny, I can't recall the colors. Why is that?

And the arrows? Yes, all the arrows but one are through him and into the tree. Many of them? Six, at least. One, I remember, is in exactly the same place, the left side of his belly, as in the first Sebastian. Yes, but that arrow is buried now up to its feathers in him. Same arrow. The others? Through his arm and into the tree, that's one. Two others close together in his chest, their long shafts crossing. Another, against all logic, through his hipbone with only feathers and the tip of the shaft remaining. And the last? Only white feathers. In his groin.

What about his face? Which one? The early face on the small head with its monumental body? Yes, that face. There is a question in his eyes. One suspects his lips tremble. And the other face? No question. No trembling. The tip of a flame, flaming.

The sun must have gone down without my noticing it. I felt cheated. Damn. What if the sun's rays don't hit this cell as they did the other? They must. Davy next to me had a sunset yesterday. Damn. What a loss. All that playing around in your head when important things are happening.

Playing around? You hit it then, Self, I said to myself. You still haven't looked at the letter. How long are you going to put it off, anyway? I missed the sunset, don't you understand? The sun will rise tomorrow morning as it always does. It will set again tomorrow evening. But that's twenty-four hours, days, years from now. Well, what do you want? You can't reach out and bring it in, can you? No, I can't. And it can't come sliding up from under the door and that whole outside world the way that letter did, either.

You're not being very objective. I don't feel objective. I need the sun. You need letters, too. I do? I'm as isolated from the one as from the other. Poor boy. Your shattered psyche is hanging

unnoticed on so many mailboxes on the street. Who can understand you? Well, isn't it true? It's like playing tennis in the dark
without knowing if your opponent is really on the other side
of the net. You keep sending ball after ball, letter after letter,
and no returns are forthcoming, no answers to questions. All
those weird shots, tremendous saves, and no response. No one
to even call out "Love" or whatever the score might be.

How am I to understand them? We are opposed. They are
not in here nor do they understand how I think and feel. You are
not out there to understand how they think or feel. What they
think I am thinking is not what I'm thinking. What they project
as my desires are only their projections. They are not my desires.
Nor do you see as they see their projections. Your desires can
only be your desires. Would you have them you, too? What was
it Earl told you? The story about the carpenter who berated his
helper for not being good enough, not being like him. The
carpenter's partner spoke up and told him that if God wanted
two of you he'd have made twins.

I had been walking so long in the same direction that I was
conscious of being dizzy. But I did not change directions.
It became rather strange. I felt as if I were walking the rim
of some crater. If I deviated the slightest from my well-worn
path, each step meeting a familiar spot on the floor, I sensed I
would fall into some abyss, and I knew I would certainly fall.
Stay straight and true, I told myself. I wondered how long I
could keep it up. But the dizziness gradually ceased or I became
accustomed to it, and I was able, after that, to walk that rim
calmly, and put my feet where they must be put to keep me from
falling.

I could read that letter now, I said to myself. And without
disturbing my circular motion around the cell, I picked up the
letter from where it rested on top of the mountain, and, still
walking, now no longer conscious of my path but confident that
I had it down pat, I opened the letter and read its contents.

The letter was from a woman on the West Coast whom I had
never met. Her husband, a dentist, worked for Cesar Chavez and
the farm workers in Delano. He operated out of a trailer con-
verted into a clinic on the Forty Acre development the farm

The Hole / 107

workers had constructed outside of Delano. She knew of me
through my articles on the farm workers in *The Catholic Worker*.
In the first few months of my jail term, I received a number of
Jewish holiday cards from her. After the third card I decided
she might want to correspond with me. So I went through the
red tape necessary to secure her on my correspondence list. Her
cards, being cards, were allowed inside; had she written in the
beginning, her letters would have been sent back marked "Not
Authorized." She kept me in touch with developments in the
grape strike and negotiations. She wrote long informed letters
and did not neglect to write about her family, which to me was
as refreshing as the latest breakthrough in the strike.

She's followed me into the "hole." Delightful. But more
delightful than that, hilarious in fact, was her request. I could
not maintain my rim walking. My movements were too energetic.
To hell with the abyss, I said to myself. I began dancing on the
island. So weird. So fucking outasight. It was ironical. Totally
incongruous. Yet, how right! How in harmony with this crazy
scene. It was too much. I collapsed laughing on the mountain.
The mountain! I said to myself, Self, you are out of your head.
You are mad.

She wants to do my natal horoscope. She's completed a course
in Natal Astrology. She wants the date and hour of my birth.
She wants to do my chart. What indeed will be my future?
How about this crazy present? Who forecast it? Was it, too, in
the stars?

I knew nothing about astrology. In fact, I still carried all
the old prejudices, some acquired (it's a "pseudo-science"),
some traditional (revolving around the fat old ladies at news-
stands pouring over some 25-cent pamphlet). But all the old
prejudices seeped out of my cell under the door as that letter
had come in. I was a believer. In what I had no idea.

My horoscope? Who cares? It couldn't really matter. What
I've made of this life could never have been forecast. Where
I have taken it, where it is now, squatting cross-legged in a
solitary cell, was not in any stars, I thought. It's all my own
weird doing. I'm totally responsible for it. No sense now, thirty
years into it, looking back to see where it should have gone,

where it might be were I not in here. I'll ride it out in my own cart behind my own strangely yoked beasts. Who knows? Maybe I would not like what she would have to say. Nonsense.

I wonder. And I was up pacing the cell again. Better than a horoscope of me—I know exactly where I am, can't really get out of it—better than that, much better for me, would be a horoscope of my son.

My son.

It had finally broken through. After three weeks of steady relentless rain, driving hard against the windows of the corridor, driving in the morning, at noon, and through the night, driving in my sleep and against me when I walked to work, driving, pouring down out of the black busy sky, the thunder rolling down the mountain and roaring through the valley, the lightning crashing above the glowing red lights of the towers on the mountaintop—for three solid weeks in late July and early August of 1969 that storm crashed about my ears, soaked my clothes and shoes, kept me inside the dorms at Allenwood—half crazed with worry, half mad with fear.

But the sun broke through. On a Sunday morning in early August. The sun made it. But not without a struggle. On that morning I walked for the first time down the pasture road to the church and cemetery. For the first time in three weeks I got away from the shouts, the fights, the constant raps, the dominoes, and the TV.

The sky was bulging with clouds, black and huge, that rolled across the roof of the valley in hulking, ponderous movements as the sun shown steadily over Penny Hill. The clouds seemed mobilized by some crazed general. They seemed determined to roll over the sun, smash it perhaps, smother it with blackness. On and on, the next one larger, more deadly than the last. Never had I seen such action in the sky, such a warring between the penetrating sun and the hulking heavy clouds massed and moving.

I had to watch that sky. I went to the old softball field and climbed the bleachers. On the top platform, already dried from the sun, I sat and looked at the sky. But it was too hard on my

The Hole / 109

neck, so I decided to lay down on that bleacher. And I did. But I felt so strange, so vulnerable there. No one else was about. Early Sunday morning. Church services going on. I had watched the bus with all of two inmates besides the driver in it heading for the stone church. Everyone else was sacked out. But it just isn't your thing to be lying down on top of a bleacher in this deserted part of camp. Not much of a bleacher either. The board was only about six inches wide and my shoulders extended over it; but it was comfortable and dry and the sky was magnificent.

The sun kept shining through, the clouds kept moving its direction, surging toward it, or so it seemed, and the sun's rays would then beat down upon me and I would no longer feel the chill I had felt while the clouds were in front of the sun. Alternately, I was warmed and then chilled, warmed and then chilled. Alternately, the air and all things about me would be clear, distinct, shining in the soft rays of the sun. The mountainside was a dappled green. Then the clouds massed again. A shroud over everything. Leaves lost their color. The fields suddenly died. The green mountain slowly darkened until it was heavy and black.

Then the sun would blaze forth again to meet my surging psyche, storm-tossed yet grateful, bitter yet accepting that warmth, biting on my confinement yet yielding to this healing as it struggled so gracefully with the dark clouds massed against it.

Yes, yes, yes.

That evening I was called to the office for a telephone message. I was told that my wife had delivered a boy at ten o'clock that morning. With some encouraging words, I had left my wife pregnant in the courtroom after my sentencing. We were all sentenced to three years.

Words, words, words. That was a long one. Try it. A poem:

To My Wife

The liberal types
from California
asked you

"What do you think this sentence will do
to the relationship you and Jack share?"
Briefly you answered
(silently noting how
comfortably they sat)
a soft word escaped you

A child is born unto us

Into that naked soupkitchen
students of hunger and need
play sadly the game of survival
by gutters strewn with a moment's release
the bottle broken and the headless toy
on hard benches and crawling chairs
spittled coat, urine-black crotch
wipers wash the stench from the eyes
men bent on home away
from the wrecked bodies of cars and men
in a house awaiting its next death
a wall-less, wardenless, wordless prison
drink finally has made it work
though Bowery down they are minds away
life complains in the drowning cells
ease has departed the stricken city
pain stalks in every part
muscles no longer master a move
the neardead and wounded tear
at the health of the passerby
infect the strong, take the crutch from the weak
so all might meet at the black edge
equal, alone, and naked

A child is born unto us

Into this neon-lit corridor
nobody's unhigh anyschool
unengaged charade of suburbia
by pastel bunks and lockers
"One sheet and a pillowcase only"

Two Army blankets and a meal sack
near a john with super-flush toilets
lane of lovelorn after dark
water fountain turned frigidaire
to the march of dominoes' clack
the din of perpetual TV
shiny-clap-heel-clop of shower pads
Puerto Rican word wargames
Black slang's dark caress
Time turns the mute ear
unargued, unidled it stays
near sockets plugged with stingers
instant coffee at a buzzing coil
wild heart at mail call
count, then, a chamber of curses
wrath's back, rage smothered in a mask
bootcamp without sergeants
all pretenders to the throne
red faces from a PA box
O coarse bourgeoisie cloister
your silence and rule are not mine

They asked "Do you ever feel frustrated?"

A gentle rain awakens my face
Where drops fall light breaks;
Day's disparate elements brace,
As your image my mind makes.

Delicate branches brimmed with dew
In symmetry so clear and bright;
Gently my thoughts cover you
As limbs in mist soar in the light.

A child is born

Though we abide in separate prisons,
Our days shattered by recurring pain;
Need knows no special seasons,
Alone love forges our chain.

Such suffering wed on a whirling anvil,

The Hole / 112

Amid chaos, war, and pain gone wild;
Everywhere lay the victims of overkill:

Despair darkness at the spark of a child.

I sat down on the mattress and, using the cell floor as a desk top, I wrote to my friend on the West Coast and asked her if she would do my son's horoscope and gave her his date and hour of birth. That finished, I filled my cup with water and unwrapped the piece of cake remaining from supper. What was that toast I made the night of my son's birth?

Oh, yes: May he live to dance on fire!

"You go to court," the hack said, "in a couple of hours, Cook. Be ready."

I took his paper plate of breakfast, a cup of milk and one of coffee, together with his warning, back to my mattress. Great, we got some apple slices today. So what if they're canned cooking apples? Number Ten can specials. They're good on Wheaties.

"Hey   we're going to court   today!" Dickey yelled.

"It'sabouttime," Eaton said. "Fivedaysin   the hole   andno charges   madeyet   Youguysgot   sixdays."

"Yeah   that'sright" John said. "Wehaven'teven   beentold whywe'rebeing   punished."

"Ithink   Iknowwhy," David said.

"Yes, butinthe   guidelines for   useofsegregation"   Eaton said, "aninmate   issupposedtobe   informedimmediately   of hisoffense   andthe   reason   forhispunishment   Igot   the guidelines   frommylawyer   Havethem   backatcamp."

"What   isthiscourt   allabout?" I asked Eaton.

"Thiswill   probablybe   theAdjustmentCommittee   Just Hendricks   andsomeothers," he said.

"Willwe   allgoatonce?" Jerry asked.

"No   chance," Eaton said. "Oneata   time."

"Whatareyou   gonnapleadDavy?" Jerry asked.

"Guilty!   Guilty!   Guilty!" David shouted.

"Be   carefulDavid," John said "Listen   tothecharge first."

"Iknow   Iknow," David said.

"HeyBob   Didthehack   tellyouto   getreadyfor   court?" Alex asked.

"No   hedidn't   sayanything   tome."

"Guess   we'renot   goingupthis   time," Alex said.

"We'vebeen   totheone   atAllenwood,right?" Eaton said.

"Only the five of us   whowalkedare   goingup?" David asked.

"Looksthat   wayDavy," I said. "Let's   notletthem breakusup   Okay?"

"Yeah   let'sstick   together," Jerry said.

"Either   weallgo   backor   weallstay," John said.

"Icoulddo   mywholebit   inhere," David said. "Nosilage nowetclothes   nowork."

The main door crashed open.

"Here   wego!" shouted Jerry.

The plate over Dickey's window opened.

"You ready, Wiley?" the hack asked.

"Give it to them, Dickey."

"Good luck, Dickey."

"Freak 'em out! Blow their minds, Dickey!" David shouted.

"Hey, Dickey, I see your face!" cried Jerry. And Dickey was led away toward the main door. For a brief moment through the cracks in our doors, we all caught a glimpse of Dickey or parts of him as he came out of his cell, all his small frame flashing. His feet were bare. There were holes in his T-shirt. His hair was matted and wilder than ever. Gaps between his teeth. He was grinning. He was gone. The corridor seemed suddenly empty. Into that emptiness we poured all our hopes, our anxieties. Get it all out of this cell, I told myself. No good in here. Minutes passed. Silence in the corridor.

Then we heard the main door open, steps approach. Dickey's cell opened, slammed shut.

"Rumon, you're next," the hack said.

"Here I go, Hobbit," David said as he passed by my cell, hacks on either side of him.

"Good luck, David," I said.

"Break a leg," John said. He was an actor. The main door shut and we all yelled at Dickey at once, which simply created a Babel of echoes. When that subsided, Dickey began.

"Hendrickswanted   toknow   whyIrioted   andtriedto escape," Dickey said.

"Rioted?" John asked. "Whatriot?"

"Was   heserious?" I asked.

"Damned   serious," Dickey said.

"Whatdidyou   tellhim?" Eaton asked.

"Itold him   Ithought   itwas   fun," Dickey said.

"What   was   fun?" Alex asked.

"Togodown   andsee   thepeople   atthegate," Dickey said.

"Isthat   all?" I asked.

"That's   all," he said. "Ididn'tsay   anythingwhen   he keptsaying   riotandescape."

The door opened again and David was led back and put into his cell.

"Foster, you're up," and Jerry was led out. These kangaroo courts are efficient, if nothing else.

"Whathappened   David?" Eaton asked.

"Nothing," David said.

"What   doyoumean   nothing?" I asked.

"Nothing," he said again.

"Didtheysay   you   riotedandtried   toescape?" Dickey asked.

"I don'tknow," David said. "I   wasn'tlistening."

"You   weren't   listening?" Eaton said. "Wow! How couldyou   notlisten?"

"Whatdid   yousay   David?" I asked.

"Nothing," he said.

"Whenthey   chargedyou   whatdid   yousay?" I asked again.

"Nothing," David said.

"Wow!" Dickey screamed, "You   musthave   blowntheir minds!"

"Well   whatdid   youdo   David?" I asked again.

"Ijust   satandlooked   atthem   and   rockedbackand forth   theway   Dickeydoes   Didn'tsay   anything   I havenothing   tosay   tothem."

The Hole / 115

"Toomuch," I said, "Isuppose   youwere   grinning   at them   allthat   timetoo."

"Maybe," he said. "Idon'tknow."

The door opened again.

"Cook, you're next," I heard the hack say as he passed by with Jerry.

You're going out to meet the Man, I said to myself. Hardly presentable. I quickly put on the T-shirt that I had not worn since I entered and stood quietly by the door in my slides. It opened and I stepped over the lip for the first time in a week, or so it seemed. The sensation of being free ran down my spine and flowed through my legs. I felt like prancing. Silly, Hobbit. These slides would fly.

"Give it 'em, Hobbit," David said. And I slid to the main door with the hacks. In the corridor beyond that door were more hacks and an inmate sitting on a table. Seg. orderly, I supposed. One of the hacks opened a door off the corridor and said something that I couldn't catch. The other hack squared off in front of me. He was tall and dark and thin. Rather frail, I thought, for a hack. I imagined his beady eyes devouring a customer in a car showroom or a slick department store. Strange. He was smoking a long thin cigar. Short, nervous puffs.

"Okay. Hands up," he said in a high falsetto voice.

No wonder. He really needs that cigar. He ran his fingers up and down my legs, around the inside of my pants at the waist, and felt in each pocket. I almost burst out laughing. I'm being officially molested, I said to myself. Go to it, hack. He pointed to the door and I went inside.

There was Hendricks, sitting behind a desk. Papers and manila folders were spread importantly in front of him. He motioned to a chair next to the desk. I sat down. Now I faced a semicircle of faces I did not recognize. Only one wore a uniform; the others, including Hendricks, were in civilian clothes. There were barred windows high in the wall and they were not opaque as ours were. I saw the morning light, a bit of the wall, and the sky beyond.

I was conscious of being unkempt and insecure in this new room. My toes stuck out of the slides, and I was embarrassed for

The Hole / 116

them. In a T-shirt. Part of my fly open. That's how they want you to feel, I said to myself. You're not fit to wear civilian clothes. You're dirty. Unclean. A health hazard to society.

"Okay, Cook, what about that riot at Allenwood. Tell us about it," Hendricks said. He, too, resembled a car salesman but one in an authoritarian bind. Meanness struggled with charm. He had obviously decided to take a hard line, but had difficulty managing it. Perhaps, I thought, he's just purposefully devious. The "fair" man—that's his rep. Even the Mafia buys that.

"What riot?" I asked. "I don't recall a riot. What property was damaged? Who was injured? What was burned or destroyed? There was no riot. No violence. I stood and waited for the hack to capture me. Was I rioting? The only violence that took place was done by one of your hacks who tackled Jerry. Unnecessarily, too."

"You were escaping, running out of the camp," Hendricks said.

"Escaping? If I wanted to escape in that sense, don't you think I'm bright enough to find a time other than broad daylight with you and all your men on the roads? That's absurd. Besides, you knew who we were—nonviolent C.O. types—and you knew when we left the dorm and where we were headed. We hooked into your two-way radio broadcasts from the bitch-box."

"You're in Education, aren't you, Cook?" he asked.

"Yes, I teach," I said. "And besides, we weren't running. We were walking."

"You went out of bounds," he said hastily, "and disobeyed a direct order. The statement here of Mr. McKinnis—he's the Food Administrator who was in charge of the office that day—states that he called you individually to stop . . ."

"Well, he's wrong. That statement is wrong. He did not call us individually to stop. He called one man's name, that's all."

The other faces said nothing. One of them, as far as I could tell, had not looked at me at all. This was Hendricks' game. I wondered if I should ask who these others were. That was to be Bob's gambit if he had been called up. He would have asked for a lawyer, too.

"Okay, Cook," I heard Hendricks say. "You'll come before the

The Hole / 117

Good Time Forfeiture Committee next week. This is just the Adjustment Committee. You can go now."

And I slid out the door.

"You're a mess, Hobbit," David said. "Did you appear in court like that?"

"Worse," I said, "I wasn't smiling then. Don't you ever wash, Davy? Or is that beard on your chin?"

"Look at Dickey!" Jerry cried. "He looks like a Chinaman. Those long hairs. How many, Dickey? Five, six? One for each day?"

"Hey, Jack, you've got a red mustache," Alex said.

"And you look like some renegade Rabbi," I said.

"Davy, you stink," Jerry said in a loud whisper.

"Yeah, I like it myself," David said. "Let me smell you. Ugh, you're gamey. Something die?"

"It was standing up most of the time," Jerry said, laughing.

"Rigor mortis," John said. "A stiff joint."

"Where's the Quaker?" Jerry asked.

"There's the filthy Quaker!" David cried. "Look at him. Dirty, dirty. He stinks, too," he said as he examined an armpit. "No purity left at all. I thought cleanliness was next to Quakerism. Look at that Quaker. Shame, Sherman, shame."

We had emerged. During a thaw an ice-covered stream, flashing and sparkling, breaks forth in places to arc in freedom before it once again goes under. So we came forth from our cells the next morning all at once into the corridor, blankets and sheets in our arms, so glad to see all of each other, eyes, faces, arms, and bodies, and to hear without distortion our voices. The iron doors of the pits seemed closed forever. The corridor, filled with our sounds, seemed harmless now and we stood near each other and rapped as if the long iron space was reserved especially for us.

"We all stink, we're all filthy," I said and the hack appeared and told us to follow him. Our first movements were variations on Jackie Gleason's "And away we go," followed by Dickey's flashing, David's hopping, John's long and graceful formality. It was too much.

"Hey," I cried, "Let's behave now. We're cons. Let's act like cons. For Chris' sake, we're in solitary. Criminals. Dirty, filthy cons. Let's behave."

"Yeah," Eaton said. "Where's the discipline in this army?"

"Fuck discipline!" Jerry said.

"Fuck armies!" said David.

"Put some order in our ranks, here," John said.

"Fuck order!" Jerry said.

"Fuck ranks," David said.

"Dickey, try to march," Alex said.

"Fuck marching!" David said.

"What we need is a strong leader," Eaton offered.

"Fuck leaders! Fuck strong leaders especially," David and Jerry were now a chorus.

"There's no organization," Eaton said.

"Fuck organization!" The chorus boomed.

"But the empire?" I shouted.

"Fuck the empire!" they responded.

"Be realistic!" Eaton demanded.

"Be impossible!" they ordered.

"How can we win the war?" asked Alex.

"Fuck the war!"

"Fuck the winning!"

"Filthy anarchists!" I cried.

"Fucking anarchists!" They yelled.

"Good idea," I said. "What we all need is a good fuck."

And we laughed and giggled, capered and pranced about as the guards—one behind and one in front—tried to ignore us all the way up to the second floor of the Segregation building, where we were led into a small gymnasium, given towels, soap, a razor with a locked-in blade, a metal mirror, and then we were ordered to shave, shower, and shit.

Delightful.

The hack did not appear to be in any hurry. And Eaton was making loud remarks about one hour of recreation a day according to segregation guidelines put forth by Merle Alexander, Director of the Federal Bureau of Prisons. We stripped and some shaved while others showered. It was a glad, free time.

The Hole / 119

We could look out of the windows and see the countryside stretch out for miles beyond the wall. Some of the windows were open and we took turns swallowing fresh air. It was Spring, indeed, out there and in our heads.

A gymnasium, I thought. A gym in jail. The recreation spa for segregated prisoners. This shower room. All these naked bodies of my friends. Sunshine and all that greenness out there under a blue cloudless sky. All the locker rooms of my high school sport-filled days flashed back to me. I was never so aware of bodies, I said to myself. Deprivation. Sometimes, after winning a football game, the mood was something like this. Embracing. Slapping asses. The strain of tired, tense muscles. The release of a hot shower. Yes, sometimes. But never this awareness. Of flesh not my own. That I love. Yes, love. Such flesh. Glistening. Drops of water. Yes, *Playboy's* Black nude has nothing on these bodies. It's beauty. Naked beauty. Emerging from a shower. These flesh-loving hands. Not only flesh. Not that alone. The sensibilities here. The sensitivity. Never aware of that years ago. Maybe I just had no name for it. How free we are. Yes, damn it, free. And innocent. Look at Dickey "The Worm." In a forest he'd move like that. Looks like a freaked-out satyr. It's a bloody Bacchanalia. And John—out of some Greek play. Eaton—gentle, sinewy, built to endure, like a long distance runner. David—out of El Greco by way of a Catholic seminary. Jerry—belongs on some tennis court in a New England country club. Alex—West Village orgy, strobe lights, water pipes.

"Oh, for a bottle of wine!" I shouted.

"Some red burgundy!" David echoed.

"And grapes and cheese and chicks and grass!" Jerry cried.

"Grass, some Acapulco Gold!" Alex sighed.

"Wow!" Dickey cried.

"On a beach," said Jerry.

"The waves talking to the shore," David added.

"A fire on the beach," Jerry said.

"Tambourines, guitars," Alex said.

"Let's dance," David said, and the white towel was a teasing veil and then, shortened, a Greek's neckerchief grasped by two stately naked figures, arms extended, in a circle turning slowly, gracefully, to Dickey's clapping rhythm and Alex's drumming on the toilet top.

Yes, yes, yes. Surely it is a crime to imprison these bodies, these minds.

"Okay, men," the hack said as he came to the shower room door. "There are clean sheets, towels, underwear, and socks over on that table. You'll have another half-hour in here, then you'll be put up on the third floor."

I am but a poor Bacchanal, I thought. Too easily depressed. I pissed out my party mood. So much and then so little. These petty changes. Socks, underwear, and now a toothbrush. We should be grateful, I suppose. I tire of this blanket-sheet syndrome. Where will this change take us? Just another cell. They have all the cards and they know it. My mind sags in the middle like that pile of mattresses there. To think in this way, damn it, is to lose. Hell, you're up against a system centuries old, founded by our Founding Fathers. Washington himself was into some New England jail—not as prisoner but as designer. They knew what they were about. Property, protect it at all costs. Look at this damn gymnasium. High arching windows. Carved paneling. That balcony jutting out from the third floor. Looks like some Old English Hall. Property, imposing and enduring property, imprisoning those who have no respect for it. One way to make a point. That's where all their energy went. And all our energy? Amounts to pissing on the wall. I had to tell Hendricks we were not escaping. Couldn't let him do that to us. Risking a two-year bit. He would if he could. Yet to do that is to play their game. Had to deny we were escaping. Yet escaping we were. Symbolically? Hell, it was real. What symbol? How explain that to Hendricks? Absurd. Risk psycho ward with that shit. Tell them the truth and they label you insane. Not in their interests to believe. Hendricks, hell. Who else would believe it? How is one to tell them? Can't do anything from here. These words will fork no lightning, as Dylan said.

Must not get too depressed. One hell of a lot of fun went down. That walk up here. I wonder if those walls and corridors have ever witnessed such a scene. Patience. I need the patience of Sweet Ass Donkey, that's what I need.

The Hole / 121

Jerry and David were playing basketball, but the ball was larger than the basket. They had to jump to knock it out after each shot. The ball was heavy and without much air in it. A pile of sagging mattresses about five feet high was near the basket. They climbed on top of it and sat cross-legged.

"How was it for you in the 'hole,' David?" I asked.

"Great, Hobbit. I really dig that solitude. I did yoga for hours. It was good."

"I was walking on my hands from one end of the cell to the other," Jerry said. "One time the hack opened the plate and there I was feet up in the air, bare-ass naked, standing on my hands. Freaked him out."

"Yeah, they don't dig it at all," David said. "I was doing the Wheel—you know, Hobbit, it's the one where you arch your back until you're all bent up like a wheel with only your hands and toes touching the floor—and he came by with lunch. Weird. They must think we're mad."

"You know," Jerry said, "I thought I'd have trouble with that cell. All alone, you know. I'm used to being with people. But it wasn't bad. I got into a lot of stuff in my head."

"No regrets about the walk?" I asked softly.

"Hell no, Hobbit," David said. "It was the only thing to do. We did it!"

"Yeah, Man, that was great," Jerry said. "In that field, hacks coming at me. When he came on me from behind, I thought the world ended. Big mother fucker. But only for a moment. And you and David moving out. I was high as a kite."

"We've fucked parole, you know," I said.

"So what, Hobbit?" David said. "I could do my whole bit in that cell. Should have been in there before now. Silly to be afraid of it."

"Yeah, we've done the 'hole,'" Jerry said. "The rest is gravy."

"You're looking good, Hobbit. All clean and pink," David said. "I liked that red mustache. Did you have one on the street?"

"Yes, the Mustache Rampant I had," I said. "Great in wintertime. Get to chew on the icicles."

We were all standing by the windows. The sun must have been directly overhead. It was hot and bright outside. My clean T-shirt was clinging to me. Sweat or the chill of the gym, I wondered. The road underneath, the fence of the tennis court, the net, and the fence again. It was so bright and clear I could distinguish bricks in the wall. I noticed, for the first time, that a wire was stretched above the top of the wall. It ran along the whole length until I lost sight of it and the wall. Far beyond the wall, I could see cows grazing in a green pasture.

"Well," I said. "We filled up the 'hole' with our noise. And filled up the way to this place. And this place—that ceiling must be fifty feet high—and now we're about to move on and up. I'd rather move out and away. But at least we'll be able to see the sun."

"Phase Two," Eaton said. "That's how they name the places. The 'hole' is One, where we're going now is Two. I don't know what Three, Four, and Five are."

"I think Five is the second floor," said Alex. "Psycho."

"This way, men," the hack said. "Pick up three of those mattresses there and follow me."

We followed him out into the corridor. A real Christ-figure there, I thought. A cart was in the middle of the landing. On the shelves were tobacco, soap, cups, tooth powder, paper, pencils, toilet paper rolls, a pencil sharpener. I saw Jerry tempted. But he didn't make any moves. That's best, I thought. Don't really know procedure upstairs. At the top landing we met another hack and a cart with trays of food. No more paper plates, anyway. Must be after lunchtime and that must be cold. The hack unlocked the main door. It had heavy glass on either side of it, and formed a see-through wall into the block. We walked inside. All but Alex had an end of a mattress. Cells on either side, name tags, faces behind the bars.

"They got lockers in these cells," Jerry said.

"Radios, too," David said.

"Come on, no talking in here," the hack said sharply.

We came to another glassed-in wall. Another block of cells. Lockers but no radios. Faces all black. Wonder if these are the rioters? We came to the last door.

The Hole / 123

"Okay, line up," the hack said. We dropped the mattresses and he shook us down before we entered. Good thing we left that cart alone, I said to myself.

"Eaton and Cook, in here. With one of those mattresses," the hack said. And we stepped inside our cell. Same old bit. Here we go again.

"Foster and Rumon, over here. Take it in there." And Davy and Jerry were put together in the cell next to the main door on the other side of the corridor.

"Wiley and Bach, in here. Right." They went in next to Bob and me on our right.

"Futterman, in here," and Alex had a cell to himself on our side but two or three cells down. The main door was unlocked and the cart wheeled in. We didn't even have time to settle in. Each of the cell doors had long metal pieces on the outside that could be raised to cover, not only the slot where the tray of food would obviously come through, but the barred window as well. The windows were all open, though. And the hack came by and gave us our trays of food. It was cold. But the novelty of the new cell, the daylight coming through the window, and the company of Bob made up for it. We quickly made a sofa of one of the mattresses doubled up and sat down to our lunch. Spaghetti, limp salad, cake, coffee, and bread.

"Let's save something for later," I said.

"Good idea. How about the cake?" Bob asked.

"Looks too good to me. I'd never let it last," I said.

"Let's do a bread and sugar thing," he said.

"Good, I don't use sugar anyway. Do you?"

"No. We can butter the bread, sugar it, and wrap in toilet paper," Bob said.

"Done."

We were eager to get started on making house. So we quickly finished off the salad and the cake, flushed the garbage of the cold meal down the toilet, scraped the trays, and stuck them back in the hole. They balanced by themselves on the two-inch platform; but by wedging one of the tin bowls into a middle position on the tray, we made it solid yet removable from the outside.

The Hole / 124

The cell was fairly clean. By using our old T-shirts as brooms we were able to collect the dirt in one spot and get rid of it by way of the toilet. We had two different kinds of mattresses. The old stuffed kind with twine around its edges and the newer plastic-covered kind.

"We've got string for a line," Eaton said.

"Yeah," I said. "Courtesy of Jimmy Hoffa. He works on these mattresses down in the basement. I heard they made the job especially for him. He's got a good scene down there. Makes connections easy."

By folding the mattresses in half and piling them in the middle of the cell with the blankets and sheets on top, we made ourselves a sizable mountain.

"Hey, we got a light up there," I said.

"Yeah, we need more string on the line," Bob said.

"There's going to be a glare in here with that on at night. That's a big bulb," I said.

"We could do a lampshade. What do you think?" Bob asked.

"Why not? What do we have? A shirt?"

"How about one of the cups?" Bob suggested.

"Sure, cut holes in the top, run lines—three of them—up to the fixture. We can do it. It's got to be free of the bulb or the cup will burn," I said.

"Hey, Hobbit!" I heard David call.

"Yeah, Davy? What's up?" I asked.

"It's who's below, Hobbit. Chandler and Bertolucci are on the second floor. They say they'll send us up some cigarettes, coffee, and candy later tonight."

"Great, how are they?"

"Bertolucci says he's okay. They had a hard time of it though the last few weeks. They're kind of pissed at us."

"Pissed at us?" I asked. "Why?"

"Because we didn't do anything about it," David said. "They were chained to the bunks in the hole, he says. Water poured on them. Maced. Sounds pretty bad."

"We didn't know about it. How could we do anything?" I asked.

"I know, but they're still uptight. Think we should have done something. They were brought up three days ago, given all their stuff, and put on the second floor. They got Commissary, radios, and lockers down there. That's the place to be, Hobbit."

"Yeah, well this isn't too bad either, I think. How will we get the stuff up?" I asked.

"Bert says he'll send it over to your side. You'll have to drop a line. You have anything?"

"Yeah, we got all sorts of line. A mattress full of it," I said.

"What are you doing, Hobbit?"

"We're making a lampshade for our light," I said. "Bob just extended the line over to the john, so, midget that I am, I don't have to stretch too far to turn it on."

"Great," David said. "You got a hole in your screen?"

"Do we have a hole in our screen?" I asked Bob. "Just a second, Davy." I could barely make out David's profile at his window.

"Yeah, we got a hole. But not a big one," Bob said.

"Not a big one, Davy," I said.

"Okay, I'll tell Bert to make the package small. Okay?"

"Right."

Our window was narrow and high. It was barred on the inside. The bars were painted a light green. The walls were a green, too. The window was hinged along the side. It opened and closed like a door. A ledge, actually the brick wall of the building, extended out from the bars. We had our sugar-bread stashed out there, along with our letters, paper, and pencils. Extending out beyond the ledge about six inches was a mesh screen in a heavy iron frame that formed a box over the window. Some of the interlinking sections on the bottom had been pried loose and bent back. Spoons probably. The resulting space provided a hole for a line to be dropped and a package received. Our hole was not very large and we only used it the first night. Crushed into the mesh on the sides were globs of hardened bread. A bird feeder.

"How's the lampshade?" I asked.

"Almost ready," Bob said. "Better move those mattresses."

"You'll have to stand on my shoulders," I said. "I'm a little heavier than you."

The Hole / 126

"Okay. You ready," Bob said. And, putting his foot on the thigh of my bent leg, he was up on my shoulders in an instant, and I was inching over to the middle of the cell.

"Hold it," he said. Looking out the window, I could see the large central tower of the prison. Pigeons were circling the tower. Some lighted and composed their feathers. The weight on my shoulders was more interesting than burdensome. Strange sensation. I had my hands bracing Bob's legs and could feel the strain of his balancing efforts.

"If I arch my back, you'll have more foot space on my shoulders," I said.

"Okay, let's try it," he said. And I arched my back and his feet flattened out, more or less, on my shoulders, his toes extending to my chest. With one hand braced on my spine, I found it was not an uncomfortable position. I could hear the raps going on in the corridor. Davy and Dickey. They were right across from each other. Everything seemed open. Other guys we didn't know were rapping, too.

"Hey, Hobbit," David called.

"Can't make it, David," I yelled. "Got Bob on my shoulders. He's fixing our light."

"Later, then," David called.

"How's it going?" I asked Bob.

"Still a hassle. Keeps falling down. A little more. Tired?"

"No, I'm okay," I said. "Funny, that in the 'hole' we had so little light and now with so much we want to control it."

"This'll be better though," Bob said. "We might get a book up."

The cell was bright with sunlight. I wonder if we'll get to see Phil Berrigan. He's in A and O over there. Seems absurd worrying about artificial light, I thought. But this is good, this weight. Substantial. So much going on around here. Not like the "hole." Busy, busy. Someone down in the yard was shouting to the Black in the cell next to us. He was shouting back. No, he's shouting at someone below us on the second floor. Have to keep my head together in here.

"Okay, finished," he said, and he sprang to the mattresses like a cat off a shelf.

The Hole / 127

"Well done," I said. And we tried the light out. The bottom of the cup became a bright yellow disk and a softer glow surrounded it above.

"Hey, we'll have a sun at night, too," I said.

"It'll do," he said.

"Next door! Next door!"

"Hey, Hobbit," I heard David shout.

"Yeah, David."

"Bert says he's got a pipe for you," David said.

"A pipe?" I asked.

"Next door! Next door!"

"There's another C.O. down there," David said. "His name's Dobbie. He's got a pipe."

"Well, what's Bert going to do? Give me another guy's pipe?"

"Next door! Hey, next door!"

"What did you say? I lost the last of it," David said.

"Is he going to give me another guy's pipe?" I said loudly.

"That's what he says," David replied.

"See if the guy wants to part with it, okay?"

"Okay, Hobbit."

"Next door! Next door!" Our wall was being pounded on. Thump! Thump! Thump!

"Next door! Next door!"

"Hey, Bob, we're being paged. I guess we're 'Next Door!' "

"Yeah, what is it?" I asked.

"What the fuck is wrong with you? I've been calling for ten minutes!" He was Black and now he was angry.

"Didn't make the connection. Our first trip in here," I said.

"Where you from?" he asked.

"Allenwood," I said.

"What did you do?" he asked.

"Fucked up," I said.

"Hey, yell down to that White son of a bitch below you and tell him I want some cigarettes. D'ya hear? Tell 'em Ransom. It's Ransom wants 'em," he said.

"Okay. Hold on," I said, and went over to the window.

"Hey, downstairs!" No answer. "This guy isn't answering," I

said to Bob. "What do we do?"

"I'll tell Ransom," Bob said.

"I'll keep trying here," I said.

"Hey, downstairs!"

"They got two of you in that cell?" he asked.

"Yeah, two in here. Two next door. Two across the way. And one beyond you. We're C.O.'s. We gave the Man some trouble out there."

"What the fuck did you do? Fight?"

"No. Not fight. We messed with their heads." Bob was talking as if he had known Ransom a long time. "Hey, what do you want us to do about this guy below? He doesn't answer. You sure he's down there?"

"Fucking right he's down there! Bang on the pipe!" Ransom yelled.

Bob came back to the rear of the cell.

"Gotta bang on the pipe," he said.

"Well, bang away. Must be the heating pipe. Big mother fucker of a pipe."

"It's hot, too. Why, in the summer time?"

"I begin to long for the 'hole' myself," I said.

"Next door! Next door! Next door!" Thump! Thump! Thump! "It's Ransom. Next door! Next door! Next door!"

"Wow!" Bob said. "This guy's heavy."

"Yeah," I said. "You feel up to it?" "Okay," Bob said. "Yeah, what is it, Ransom?" he said slowly.

"Tell that mother fucker if he don't send me some cigarettes, I'll burn him in the yard next I see him."

"Right," Bob said. "Let's see if we can reach him," and Bob shouted out the window.

"Hey, second floor!"

"Yeah, I hear." We heard a voice, none too eager, answer from below.

"Ransom wants some cigarettes," Bob shouted. "Asks you to send some up."

"Don't have any," came the drawling voice after a long pause.

"Hey, Hobbit," I heard David in the corridor.

"Yeah, David," I said.

The Hole / 129

"Bert says the guy Dobbie says it's okay for you to have the pipe."

"Tell him to keep it down there. Be too much of a hassle. Thank Bert and Dobbie for me. Okay?" It was already too complicated in here.

"Got it, Hobbit," David said. "I don't think Dobbie really wants to part with it, anyway. Bert's pushing a bit."

"Good. Tell 'em I don't need it. Can make it without a pipe. Been a week now. Make sure of those cigarettes, though."

"How's the guy downstairs?" I asked Bob.

"He says he doesn't have any cigarettes," Bob said. "We'll be getting some. Let's bring Ransom in on ours. How about it?"

"Sounds good to me," I said. "But it sounds to me that Ransom wants cigarettes now."

"Next door! Next door!"

"Yeah, what is it?" Bob said, still cool.

"Did you get that guy downstairs?" he asked, his voice sharp and cutting.

"Yeah," Bob said. "But he says he doesn't have any. Can't bring it up now anyway, can we?"

"Fuck the mother fucker!"

"Hey, Ransom," Bob said. "We got connections on the second floor. We're getting cigarettes in tonight. We'll take care of the butts, okay? Should be enough for everyone."

"Who you know down there?" Ransom asked, a little suspicion in his voice.

"Bertolucci and Chandler," Bob said.

"That fat small White cat?" he asked.

"Yeah, that's Bert. You know him?"

"Seen 'em in here a couple of times. Okay. Tonight, right? Eaton, your name?"

"Right," Bob said. "How many we got up here?"

"How many of you?" Ransom asked. He was relaxed, a little high, having scored. "Just the two of us before you came."

"Then there's nine," Bob said. "If we get a pack, it'll give us two each with two left over. That's cool."

"Solid," said Ransom.

Eaton moved away from the door. He was smiling. We separated the mattresses and formed two large cushions, one on either side of the cell. We both sat down.

"Little heavy," I said.

"Yeah," Bob said. "Should be all straightened out now, though. Hope Bert comes through. Going to get a pipe?" he asked.

"No, I've told them to keep it. What happened to the simplicity of the 'hole'? Damn, this isn't solitary. It's as busy as a supermarket's parking lot."

"Hey, Cook, Cook." I heard my name being called from the corridor, but I didn't recognize the voice. I went to the window.

"Yeah, what is it?" It was the guy across from us. O'Brien was printed on the card over his door.

"You want some George?" he asked.

"George?"

"Yeah, some roll-your-own. Stick your arm out. I'll throw a line over."

I tried to put my arm through the bars in the window.

"No luck," I said. "My arm won't go through." I could only get my hand and forearm out. I tried the other holes. My other arm. No luck.

"Hey, Bob," I said. "You're going to have to do the throwing and catching, looks like. My arms won't go through."

"That's your weight lifting," he said. "What good is all that, anyway?"

"Hey, O'Brien," I said. "My partner will catch it. Hold on."

"Okay," O'Brien said. "Hey," he added, "why don't I save it for tonight? We'd have more cigs, then."

"That's cool," I said.

"Okay," he said.

"Well, Bob," I said once back on my cushion, "looks like you're going to do all the hustling in this cell. Sorry about that. I'll just watch."

"Simplifies things for you, I guess," Bob said.

"It's okay with me. I think we're in solid with Ransom. And that guy O'Brien, he's ready for some ready-mades, too. We'll make it."

"Yeah, I think we got it made. It's just a totally different scene here than below. Takes some getting used to. But, damn, what a fine window we got. Good view of the yard; A and O over there with Berrigan in it. A little bit of the ball field."

"Yeah, and a whole roll of toilet paper. Toothbrushes. We'll have to get some powder. My mouth feels like someone camped on it."

"Yeah, tramped on, sort of. So is mine."

"We're lucky to have David and Dickey on either side up front. They can keep an eye out when we move things."

"Looks like we're gonna move with abandon."

"I've got to get to work on a line," Bob said.

"I'm anxious to see how it goes. Do you know how the lines work?" I asked.

"Put a weight on the bottom of a line, I guess," Bob said. "Drop it out and let gravity handle the rest."

"It's the guy below us that Bert's going to use."

"No problem. Too bad about your arm. Miss the fun."

"Watching you amuses me," I said. "You handled Ransom beautifully. Really. Sound stuff."

"One way of creating community," he said.

"In solitary, to boot," I said. "How we do fuck with them."

"Why do you think they paired us off as they did?" Bob asked. We were still on our cushions. The corridor was quiet. It was midafternoon and quite hot. We were stripped down to our shorts.

"I don't know," I said. "Who can fathom such minds? Perhaps it is simply age. We're the oldest. John and Dickey are about the same age. David and Jerry are the youngest. Alex, somewhere in between."

"Sounds almost logical," Bob said.

"Speaking of Alex, I haven't heard a word from him," I said.

"Yeah, we'll have to bring him in. He must feel cut off down there."

"It strikes me that doing a bit in here would not be all that difficult."

"Bert and Chandler seem to think it is," Bob said.

"Yeah, I don't dig some of that business. How were we to know they were in the 'hole'? And if we knew they were in the 'hole,' but knew nothing about the reasons for it, how would we proceed?"

"They seem to imply we should come running from Allenwood every time they get in trouble," Bob said.

"And I wonder about the trouble," I said. "Our experience in the 'hole' could not have been all that unique. And it went unhassled."

"Well, if I hadn't been allowed to shower and get out of that cell when we did, I would have raised a stink," Bob said.

"Agreed. But still in solitary down there, even up here, your environment is so curtailed that to fuck up really requires initiative, personal initiative," I said.

"What do you mean?" Bob asked.

"Well, look at it. Whom do you see in the 'hole' and how many times do you see them?"

"Hacks at breakfast, lunch, supper," Bob said. "And the counts."

"An administrator or two, gloating," I added.

"That's it."

"Exactly. That's it. At Allenwood or in population out there, a guy is surrounded by 350 or 1,200 men. Plus all the hacks. And some of them he cannot help but relate to. No work gangs, no TV room, no dorms in here."

"And the only times you really have to relate to hacks is when they're serving you," Bob said.

"Right," I said. "And that must be a hassle for them to handle. Did you see that scene? The hacks were running around like waitresses in a diner. And after it all they had to scrape the plates and stack them. That's rich."

"So, what do you conclude?"

"That to fuck up in here requires effort."

"Then how would you mess with them in here?" Bob asked. "Why don't we walk a bit. I'll keep a count." And we began walking around our mountain. Each fifty times around the cell. Bob would make a mark on the pipe. We walked for miles.

"If it was simply a matter of striking back—that is, not for any definable grievance, I'd do it the way we do it. Contraband, hustling, trying to make out of chaos a community. That kind of thing strikes at the root of their thing. It is to deny their thing on all levels."

"How so?" Bob asked.

"Contraband negates their punishment-by-deprivation: no tobacco, candy, coffee, tooth powder. Hustling negates their concept of segregation, throwing the bad apple out. No contacts. And community creates something positive out of segregation, creates in fact what segregation attempts to destroy."

"So, according to you, the guys who get drugs, booze, and food into jail, or move stuff in here, are more principled than political types who put on demonstrations and such," Bob said.

"Not consciously principled. I'm not saying that. I think they're more effective, that's all. And more in tune with the realities of jail. I'd say that, too."

"But what are they changing by such action?" Eaton asked. Arn't they just sustaining it by accepting it and moving within it?"

"Yes, but neither you nor I can change this system by fucking up count. Short of helping a man escape, the only real way you can help a prisoner is making his hard time good time. That means booze, pot, and good food. It has the added spice of making criminals and accomplices out of those who would help prisoners and criminals. Such goodies help a man to live as if the bloody institution doesn't exist. If it doesn't exist, it can't do us so bloody much harm. Why, do you think, the system fails so fantastically? Not because its programs are poor, brutal, and but rhetoric—they are that; but because within prison one is forced into, or one adjusts to, the same kind of criminal activities that got one in here in the first place. No change in men. Just think what a drag our society would be if prisons succeeded in turning out the kind of men they purport to do?"

"Yet you seem to be ruling out any effort, from the inside, to effect change," Bob said over his shoulder.

It was a strange scene. At times I'd be walking and talking as if alone. Then, turning a corner, we'd be abreast of each other. Finally, I'd be following him and watching as he counted off on his fingers, his hands clasped behind his back.

"Not really," I said. "We wouldn't be here if that were the

case. I'm thinking of guys in this joint or Atlanta, who are looking at fifteen, twenty, forty years. Guys with ten on twenty or double life, for God's sake. Guys who'll never know another. All their springs, summers, falls will be in jail. All of it, perhaps, winter in the head, if not in the yard. I don't think we have a right to fuck with that way of life. As cons they have a certain community, they have ways of getting things and fulfilling needs that the administration either does not know about, ignores, or is helpless to do anything about.

"So, even homosexuality can be understood—it's in fact perfectly natural—if a man is going to be among men for the rest of his life. What's the difference, after all? If the sun is going to rise and set on a man in jail, if the seasons are going to change but find that man in jail still, then that jail is his world to do with as he can, make out of it what he will, given the limitations."

"You're arguing the status quo," Bob said.

"No, that's a term applied from without and from above. I'm arguing the life style of prisoners. That's within and down. In opposition to what the powers-that-be would make it or believe it to be."

"Well, you seem to be accepting, acquiescing, to a prisoner's life style, a fancy term for suffering, I think, without trying to ease his pain any, make it a little more comfortable for him," Bob said.

"Well, that sounds a little pious to me. One of the pious folk at the *Worker* quoted Brecht to me to the effect that I should not let 'my cigar go out in bitterness,' which prompted me to reply, 'Nor my pipe in piety.' I don't think bitterness extinguishes flames, anyway, as piety (the wrong kind) surely does; but then I don't know the context of Brecht's sentence—don't know how he stuffed his word, so anyone's peeling of it is strictly his own."

"But it's a social structure, a prison, we're talking about. We should be trying to change it. And if we can't change it immediately, then we can work for changes within it that'll be for the benefit of prisoners. That's what this friend of mine is going to do for us and for all prisoners."

"So much reform, so many good intentions!" I cried. "The system is built to accommodate them. They already have *pious*

The Hole / 135

chaplains, *understanding* caseworkers, programs of *rehabilitation* and entertainment. Here and on a national scale. Our space program is just entertainment for the masses while it opens up a new frontier for the Pentagon. Behind the platitudes of our astronauts there was a simple declaration of war."

"You see, it's not only prisons, damn it. We live our fucking lives out within social structures—colleges, movements, ghettos, jails, this fucking empire—all jails in a sense; but God or somebody help us if that is all we live within; if we are defined and contained solely by these spleen-spawned, inept, asinine, eyesores; if we are so poor in necessity that Nixon and his minor league counterparts are the only pint-sized antagonists around; if we can, in fact, be destroyed by them; if they do not function simply as negative terms in the equation of our life; if they are not mere idols of man that measure the men who bow to them—"

"Yes, meanwhile the prison goes on," Bob said, "and everything remains intact. Goliath still stands. And he continues to oppress men, fuck up the environment, and lead us on to World War III."

"True enough," I said. "They will not fall by my puny efforts. And perhaps they will not even change. Take Allenwood. Thirty years ago that place would have been unthinkable. It stands today, even to skeptical critics, as a showpiece of U.S. penology. About fifty years behind the enlightened socialist countries, it is true, but nonetheless for America it is, objectively anyway, a sign of reform and adaptation to more liberal trends in penology. But I can bear witness, you too, Bob, along with a lot of those other guys, mostly mute, to the Sing Sing nature of the place in times of crisis. It out-Sing-Sings Sing Sing at those times really, for without bars and containing walls, in apparent freedom, unchained, potentially (a little hill away) away, the prisoner must construct these necessities himself, discover them where they do exist—implanted there by liberal laws—in his mind, if he is to endure his troubles without going berserk or lengthening his confinement. Bars, like these, would be healthy to grasp; walls, like these, might serve to batter our heads against. But that token freedom! The gates locked by prisoners!"

"Let's change directions," Bob said. And suddenly the room

was whirling by in a different fashion. I hadn't talked so much in a week or more. It felt good somehow. Let it all out.

"There have been changes. Such changes. For the better, most would say. But it is still prison, willy-nilly of changes. The stripes and welts may no longer appear so frequently on the backs and shoulders of prisoners; but they are terribly apparent on the psyches that suffer them in these reformed institutions. And are you telling me there will be an end to jails through reform? I think not. Those guys with life sentences running consecutively, 'running away' as they say, they know it will not be so. So they adjust to that necessity. And that adjustment, their social life within walls, is not something I have any right to seek to change. Thus I am reluctant to disturb their patterns. As on the Bowery, that other jail, the struggles I admire go on within such a context, the victories I applaud are won despite it, and the men so inflamed are not measured nor are they contained by the institutions they inhabit."

I had worked up a sweat. Bob, too. Our shorts were soaked. No need to wash. My feet ached from the walking and the constant turning. Our pace had been much faster than that in the "hole," at least for me. We separated the mattresses, sat down, and waited for supper.

"Quite a sermon," Bob said.

"Sermon, shit," I said. "Leave that for the priests. Your Quaker meetings, too. Piety, how I dread the word. It's as bad as 'virtue'—all that pseudo-sanctity and complacent righteousness. Did you hear my line on the preacher at Allenwood with his damned banjo, guitar, mouth organ, and silly putty?"

"No. What is it?"

"What do preachers do when they can't preach?" I asked.

"Tell me, I have no idea," Bob said laughing.

"They annoy in other ways," I said. "Zorba was right, I think, to spit at the sight of one and ask for his curse. And Blake defined Prudence (and all her relatives) once and for all."

"But it's a kind of inner conversion," Bob said, "an inner almost religious experience you've been raving about."

"Agreed," I said, "but inner change need not stink of devotion to some institution's god or loyalty to all the goody virtues of pious folk. The 'change' I speak of is what happens to wood when put in fire. Ammon Hennacy, who died last January at 75, and his One Man Revolution. He spoke only in terms of the revolution within individual men and the constant, ruthless struggle within himself. He told me, the last time I saw him, that it wouldn't end until his death. He might yet cop out, he said. And that after a lifetime of resistance, going back to when he was a C.O. during the First World War with Alexander Berkman in Atlanta, through World War I, the Catholic Worker movement, nonpayment of taxes, protest against World War II, the Civil Defense bit in New York City. He and Dorothy began that protest, and they kept it up after repeated jailings until the rest of the movement came in on it. And those blackouts stopped. 'This House Has No Bomb Shelter.' And he was still picketing and fasting— forty days the year before he died—every year at tax time.

"He was on his way to the courthouse, his sign on his shoulder, when the walls of his heart cracked. Probably out of glee. Couldn't have been bitterness. Hell, it was both. Too much of both.

"There was a Revolution, I think. And an Incarnation, if you will: that word became flesh. And that structure, Ammon's life and work, was erected daily over the abyss. A 'social' structure, too, for all of us must look at it and be ashamed. And in the last analysis, government, church, courts, and law figure in that structure solely as names on protest placards now idle against Ammon's wall."

"Hey, Hobbit," I heard David call.

"Yeah, Davy."

"You should see the sunset. Too bad you're over there," he said.

"Yeah, I know. I wish I were there, too," I said.

"It's outasight!" he said.

"Well, we have a mighty sky out our window anyway. I was just looking at it. Black over crimson and brilliant orange stretched and silky."

"See you," David said and he went back to watch the sun.

The Hole / 138

Standing by the window, my back to the pipe, I watched the darkness descend beyond my hand and the bar it grasped. The end of the day. Where are they all now? In what rooms? What apartments? Do they have friends over for supper? We eat so early in here. It's just suppertime out there. Our evening is about over. Theirs is just beginning. These cells are strange. I see David at that window and when he leaves I feel as if he's never to return to that place. I wish my thumb could hold that darkness up. Right there, stop it. No chance. See, it goes down regardless. This day will never come again. Ended. And this year? Where can I find it? Somewhere beyond that darkness there. That will not cease to descend. Gone. John and Dickey are laughing. What's it all about? "Not while I'm in here"—Is that what John said? Ransom's laughing, too. One day of joy. Backed up by a year of pain. No regrets, they said. I wonder. Two months from now? Six months more. No parole. No regrets? What do the French say? Everything falls, everything breaks, everything dies. Something like that. Everything's like that. No strength in your thumb, poor Hobbit. You grow older, and weaker, and no wiser.

"Hey, Jack," Bob said from the front of the cell. "The hacks coming again with a cart, sounds like."

"I wonder what it's all about," I said.

The main door of our block opened and a hack came in, his cart filled with goodies. He began distributing them to David and Dickey.

"Let me see," I said. "Hey, he's got small cups, and soap, and toilet paper. Paper and pencils. They're new ones. There's some Buglar on the bottom shelf. Should we make a play for some?"

"Nothing lost," Bob said. "What else does he have? We need tooth powder, first of all. Use some more soap. I used what we had for a weight on my line," he said in a whisper.

"Okay, men," the hack said.

"You were out at Allenwood a while ago, weren't you?" I asked.

"Yeah, going out again, I hope," he said.

He was a young, smiling hack. But he had a bad rep. His thick black hair in a crew cut. Still no forehead, I thought. His gray uniform bulged with last night's beer. Face is red. Maybe tonight's beer. He must be just starting his shift. Imagine him at a bar, country-western on the jukebox, loud hee-haw laughter. We are the butt of many of his jokes, I bet.

"What'll it be, tonight?" he said. Must be his standard line, I thought. Not very swift.

"We need tooth powder, soap, paper and envelopes, and toilet paper," Bob said.

"Okay, here's the powder."

"Just that much? A little cup?" I asked. "That's enough for about two teeth. We must have at least fifty between us, right, Bob?"

"Sorry," he said. "Here's your soap."

"But there are two of us. You expect us to share one small bar of soap?" Bob said.

"Just two sheets of paper and two envelopes?" Bob asked.

"That's it," he said. "You don't have any friends out there anyway," and he laughed. That's a con's laugh, I thought. A con's joke, too. There isn't really much of a difference.

"He likes to pretend that he does," I said.

"Yeah, I'm a great pretender," Bob said.

"How about some toilet paper?" I asked.

"Coming up," he said, and he grasped a roll as if it were a softball and slammed it up against the wall. It made a loud, echoing sound. Bob and I looked at each other. He likes that sound. Power. Then he lowered the outside plate until the slot appeared and shoved the flattened toilet roll through it.

"Not bad," I said. "Some Buglar could come through there, too."

"Not on this block, it doesn't," he said.

"How about a couple of pencils?" Bob asked.

"Okay, want 'em sharpened, too, I guess," the hack said.

"Yeah, my teeth hurt from gnawing on the one I got," I said.

"That's it, men," he said, and he rolled his cart down in front of Ransom.

"It's about time we got some of this stuff," Bob said. "Do you know what the guidelines say about segregation?" he asked.

"No, tell me," I said. "But, first, let's decide who brushes his teeth first. My mouth feels worn and ragged, like an old pair of dungarees."

"Okay, why don't we divide this stuff up? We have more cups now."

"Why not just pour some out for tomorrow morning? And we'll splurge on the rest right now."

"Good idea. For that you get to go first," Bob said.

"I thank ye," I said.

"Thou art welcome," Bob said.

"I'll be a bloody Quaker soon myself," I said with a mouthful of brush and powder-suds.

"How does it feel?" Bob asked.

"Like dawn," I said, as I splashed my face with water. "And a brisk wind. With such a mouth I could even sail into society."

"We had powder like this on the *Phoenix*," Bob said. "I'll have to tell you about that."

"When I used to teach at Hobart, Griff and I would go out sailing after faculty meetings. On Seneca Lake. Faculty meetings make you sterile. Seemed like after every meeting, there would be white-capped water and high winds on the lake, and as all the other boats would be docking, Griff—such a beautiful man—and I would tack her out. Too much."

"Aren't we supposed to get a Bible in here? Or haven't we reached that phase of rehabilitation yet?" Bob asked.

"Can't be trusted with the Holy Word," I said.

"Why don't I ask him?" Bob said.

"Too late," I said. "He's done taken the goodies away."

"Not bad. Not bad at all. We got more soap, so we don't have to worry about using our weight to wash with. Two rolls of toilet paper. If we squeeze this one in here between the sink and the wall, like so. *Voilà!* A shelf. And here's our community drinking cup to put on it. Now we've got two small cups for the coffee—let's hope—we get tonight. And tomorrow's powder. New pencils. Wish I had this in the 'hole.' Writing on this paper with a stubby pencil brought back my grade-school days. My brother and I went to a Quaker school. Very strict. We'll keep our supplies out on the ledge. What if we use one of these blankets as a bath mat? It'll soak up the water we splash around."

"Good idea," I said. "We need a rug in here."

"There," Bob said. "Folded it fits wall to wall. Now, how about a walk until it gets really dark and then we can begin to bring up some other goodies."

"Should we turn our sun on?" I asked.

"Why not? The light bill is not ours," he answered.

"Neat little house we have here," I said. "Almost comfortable."

"Yeah, clean and contented. Not bad for solitary."

"How far did we walk this afternoon?" I asked.

"Let me check. I think a little over a mile," he said. "Yes, a mile and a quarter. Should we finish off the second mile? I think we have time."

"Sounds good to me. You start or should I?"

"I'll begin this time."

"How sweet it is," I said.

"Hey, Hobbit," David was calling.

"Yeah, David."

"Bert says they'll be ready in about an hour. Says he's sending up a love letter, too. He's really high down there."

"A love letter?"

"Yeah, he and Chandler both are writing. Wait a minute. He's shouting something up. What is it, Jerry?"

"Bert's sending up a love letter," I told Bob.

"Why not?" Bob said. "I'd like a love letter from Bert."

"Hey, Hobbit, it's NEWSTIME," David yelled.

"Newstime?"

"Yeah, they got radios down there," David said.

"Do you feel like hearing the News?" I asked Bob.

"Not especially," Bob said.

"Hey, David," I said. "We don't especially want to listen to the News. Do you? Why don't we just spend a quiet night at home in our cells. We don't need all that gore in here, do we?"

"You're right, Hobbit. I'll tell Bert to save it for tomorrow. Okay?"

"Right," I said.

Night, black and starless, settled down on the prison. It covered all the buildings, eliminated all the lines and angles, and blanketed the yard. Like some huge black hen brooding on its strange eggs, night came and covered all the separate

The Hole / 142

cells, filled with pacing, swearing, laughing, or silent men. It spread its dark wings over the outer walls and, by the window, I felt the warm breeze of the wings folding. A gentle night, I thought. The breeze is soft yet it moves. On the surface of a lake you could hear the ripples. On such a starless night in that ragged sleeping bag on the tenement rooftop—she and I—surrounded by the black shapes of chimneys—she and I—under that deep and dark and vast sky— We—

Yes, yes, yes.

And we woke to the gawking of teenagers on the rooftops across the street.

"Hey, third floor," I heard a voice from out of the darkness below me.

"Yeah, you ready?" I asked.

"Drop your line. But watch out for the light," he said.

His voice seemed much more alive now than this afternoon. A quiet excitement in it. I was a little anxious, too. Contraband is no small matter, I thought. If we get caught, it's back to the "hole." On their terms. The spotlight. Like in the movies. See how it hits the windows over there. Each window. Top to bottom. Over the roof. Down again. I wonder where it is anyway? Batman should appear. If it stopped over there, I could maybe make an eagle with my hands. No luck. Light has to be behind you.

"Hey, Bob, he's ready downstairs," I said.

"Okay, let me get next to that window."

"Watch the light," I said.

Bob unwound his line. It was about twenty feet long. At one end, tied all around, was our bar of soap. He dropped it through the hole. Something like ice fishing.

"Does he have it yet?" I asked.

"Not yet. There—now he has it," Bob said.

We watched the bouncing ball of light.

"What's the song tonight?"

"Yeah, I was thinking the same thing. Like in the movies when I was a kid. Saturday matinee. What do you think it is? 'John Henry'?"

"Sounds good," I said. "Know it?"

In low soft voice, Bob sang:

> John Henry told his captain,
> "A man ain't nothing but a man,
> And before I'd let that steam-drill beat me down,
> I'd die with this hammer in my hand."

"How about 'Big Rock Candy Mountains'?" I said.
"Let's see," said Bob:

> In the Big Rock Candy Mountains,
> All the cops have wooden legs,
> And the bulldogs all have rubber teeth
> And the hens lay soft-boiled eggs.

"Hey, he's tugging at the line," Bob said.
"Haul him in," I said.

> The farmer's trees are full of fruit,
> And the barns are full of hay.

"Hey, watch the light," I said. "Is it stopping?"
"No, there it goes again," Bob whispered.

> In the Big Rock Candy Mountains,

He was hauling the line in slowly and I was winding it up
as it came in behind him. I was humming along.
"Maybe we got a soft-boiled egg," I said.

> The jails are made of tin,
> And you can bust right out again,

"Here it is," he said.

> As soon as they put you in.

"Will it come through the 'hole'?" I asked.

The Hole / 144

"Yeah, gotta squeeze it in," he said.

"Midwife to the Night," I said. "What would the Society of Friends say about that?"

"They'd dig it," Bob said. "Here it is. Hey, second floor, we got it okay. Thanks."

"There's more," came the voice. "Drop your line again."

"This is too much," I said.

Bob untied the package and stashed it under his mattress. Then he dropped the line again.

"What'll it be now?" I asked. "That was a charming performance you gave there."

"How about 'Gee, But I Want To Go Home,'" he said.

"An oldy, but a goody," I said.

> The coffee that they give us,
> They say is mighty fine,
> It's good for cuts and bruises
> And it tastes like iodine.

> I don't want no more of army life,
> Gee but I want to go,
> Gee, but I want to go home.

"That ball isn't following in time," I said.

"Taking him longer this time," Bob said. "Wonder if anything's wrong."

> The clothes that they give us,
> They say are mighty fine,
> Me and my buddy
> Can both—

"Here he is," Bob said.

> . . . fit into mine.

> They treat us like monkeys

The Hole / 145

We sang as he hauled in the line.

> And make us stand in line,
> They give you fifty dollars a week
> And take back forty-nine.

"Got it," Bob said. "It's heavier than the first one."

> I don't want no more of army life,
> Gee, but I want to go,
> Gee, but I want to go home.

"Thanks, second floor. Good night," Bob said.

"Let's see what Bert and Rich have sent us," I said, as we crouched over the packages. I felt an old excitement. Christmas day. The tree all but hidden with presents. Mom and Dad.

"Hey, there's a pack of Camels. Lots of coffee. This must be powdered milk. And candy."

"This must be the love letter," I said, as I picked up the small square-shaped wad of paper. They did a job folding it. What's this? Hey, Tang. The orange juice of astronauts."

"Here's some George. Rotten tobacco," Bob said.

"It is tobacco, though," I said. "But as bad as the real George."

"Matches. Good we got a pack of them. Two each again. Let's tell the others what we got."

"Hey, everyone," Bob yelled out the window. "We made a score. Got cigarettes, coffee, milk, Tang, candy, George, and matches. Now who wants what?"

"Candy for me and Jerry," David yelled. "I'll thank Bert and Rich."

"I'll have some Tang," John said.

"Coffee with milk," said Dickey. "And some cigarettes."

"We can each have two cigarettes and some of the George," Bob said. "Two matches, too."

"Hey, Eaton," David called to Bob. "Bert says he'll get a book up tomorrow night. He says we only got an hour before count, so we'd better hurry up. Did you get the note? Oh, he said they sometimes sneak around before count, too."

The Hole / 146

"Yeah, we got it," I said. "We'll send it over. It's all folded up."

"A couple cigarettes is fine with me," O'Brien said.

"Me, too," said Ransom.

"Up to you," Bob said. "There's enough coffee, I think."

"Look," Bob went on, "why don't I just take out for Jack and me, Ransom and Alex, and send the rest on to you, John. Then you can throw across to Davy and Davy over to O'Brien."

"I can get to O'Brien easier from here," Ransom said.

"Okay, we'll do it that way. I'll make up the packages."

"Hey, Hobbit, what kind of candy is it? Jerry wants to know."

"It's butterscotch hard candy. You know, the kind wrapped up in cellophane."

"Yeah, they're good."

"You and Dickey better keep a watch on the door when Bob throws. Can you see much of it?"

"I can see down the corridor about two cells," David said.

"So can I," Dickey said.

"You ready, John," Bob said. "Got your goodies coming. Hey, I kept the extra cigarettes. Okay? If we get a pack tomorrow night, one of you get it."

"Throw the end with the weight," said O'Brien. "It's easier."

"Okay. John, you got your arm out? David, you watching?"

"All set."

"Twirl it," O'Brien suggested. "Hold it about two feet from the weight and twirl it and let fly."

"I see. Yeah. Here it comes, John."

"Missed, too low," John said.

I watched Bob. His arm was through the bars to the bicep. He pulled his line in.

"Not as easy as one might think," he said.

He tried again. I could see the white piece of soap go round and round with a whirring sound and then disappear out of sight, like a flying bird.

"Too high that time," John said.

"You gotta watch out for that runner up there," O'Brien said. "See it? That metal piece goes right along the top of the cells. That's for opening them from the front. A line can get caught up there easy." O'Brien was from New York City.

The Hole / 147

"Ready, John," Bob said. "Here it comes."

"Got it!" John shouted.

"Great, Eaton," David called.

"Good shot," O'Brien said.

"Pull it in, John," Bob said. "I have the package up."

"And there it goes," I said. "Well done."

"Now for Ransom's package," Bob said.

"You have two lines?"

"Yes, we got two lines. This one's shorter, though."

"You do take precautions," I said. I was sitting on our huge mountain. The white sheets under me were cool and I was quiet and comfortable.

"Hey, Davy," Bob called. "I put the note in John's package. After you and Jerry read it, send it back to John and then to me. Okay, John? We haven't read it yet. That way I'll get my line back, too."

"Okay. After count?" David asked.

"Yeah, after count," Bob said. "Ransom, you ready?"

"I'm cool," said Ransom, and again the whirring sound of feathers beating and another white bird flew down the corridor.

"Our other bar of soap didn't just go flying away, did it?" I asked.

"No, Ransom's package was smaller, so I wrapped and tied it tightly and sent it down," Bob said.

I could hear David and Jerry laughing and giggling in anticipation.

"Your arm's almost long enough to reach over here," David said.

"That's not all that's long over there," Jerry said. "Right, Dickey?"

"Try again," Ransom said. "You went wide." His tone was helpful.

"Here it goes."

"Got it," Ransom said. "I got my own line. You can pull yours in." His voice was rich and dark. That dark caress again.

"Good," Bob said.

"Okay," said Ransom. "It's all yours. Thanks, Man. Be ready in a minute, O'Brien."

The Hole / 148

"That's cool. We got time."

"Well," Bob said, "if you get off your throne there, we can make the beds up and be all ready for count."

"Throne, hell," I said. "I'm on a mountain. Snow-capped as you can see. And a much higher mountain than I've been on in a week. But then I had a green island. No island here. This mountain rises out of the sea. Has levels, some plateau there about the middle. And look where I was sitting—in a white crater. No volcano. Must be a lake at the top of the mountain. What do you think?"

"I think you were sitting on my sheets," said Bob.

"Okay, let's make the beds," I said. "How should we arrange them?"

"If we put them side by side horizontally, it might get a little stuffy so close in this weather, and one of us would have to step over the other to get to the john," Bob said.

"Vertically, we still have almost the same problem," I said.

"What if we stagger them vertically? One up near the door, the other back here. That would give us room to walk as well."

"Sounds good to me. We'd be the greatest distance, too, from each other's, as well as our own, feet. Which do you prefer, the door or the window?"

"Window's fine with me."

"Done. Let's do it."

"First, why don't you work on the matches. We have four. Tearing them in half will give us eight pieces."

"Okay," I said.

Carefully, I opened and split the cardboard end of each match and, holding on by the ankles, I gently spread so slowly her legs until her round head just trembled with pleasure and burst with a sigh in half to lay quietly on her side, now exposed, halved, at last to be shared.

"Here are the matches," I said. "Have you read much of Sartre?"

Bob hid the eight pieces of match in different folds of the toilet paper roll. He stashed the candy, coffee, some George wrapped in toilet paper, and five cigarettes under his mattress.

The Hole / 149

He hid the "striker," a quarter of the matchbook's striking surface, in the crack between the john and the wall.

"No, you said you had his trilogy out at camp. I want to read that."

"He has a section about 'holes' in *Being and Nothingness*. I've seen it printed elsewhere with the title 'The Hole.' " I said. "He reduces everything to 'holes' and how we relate to them. You know, food, sex, being, and nothing—that's a hole, see? It is and it isn't."

"I don't follow," Bob said.

"Well, he uses the expression 'the obscenity of the feminine sex'—I think that's it. And that obscenity he says is because she's a hole, a gaping hole. And eating is obviously a matter of filling a hole; shitting, matter coming out of a hole; talking, hole to hole; kids play constantly with holes; dying, you're put into a hole. All holes."

"Okay, so what's the point?"

"Sartre concludes that essay called 'The Hole' by saying—I'll never forget it—he says, 'Man is a useless passion.' "

"So?" Bob asked.

"So? He's wrong," I said.

We made our beds and were sitting cross-legged on them when the hack came by to count. I was much relieved after the haste and excitement of the catching and throwing business; I was relieved, too, to get that stuff out of our cell. They could break the group apart on a silly bust like that. But the risk is necessary. It's the only rational response to this situation.

Good thing we got Bert and Rich downstairs. Not complete strangers in here. So much hustling over coffee and cigarettes. At home in Allenwood, never thought about it. What home? You lost that home. And you've tarried here a week now. And who knows when or where you'll be going next? They could transfer us all over the States if they wanted to. Could go out tomorrow. On a Sunday? No chance. I'm glad my arm is too large for that window. That's a hassle, I think. Bob digs it though. He'll soon master it. Perhaps throw to two cells at a time or something. Thanks to Bert and Rich, I can fill my yearning lungs with tobacco smoke. Haven't had a pipe now in six days. That's as

The Hole / 150

long as I've ever gone without a pipe. Two cigarettes. And some George. A piece of candy. And coffee, I almost forgot the coffee. That'll taste good right now. Yet I am uneasy. I wonder why? Perhaps that letter from Bert and Rich. I didn't want to open it. Wonder why? John and Dickey have read it by now. No sound from them. And David and Jerry must have it in their cell. No rap, no sound?

"Hey, Hobbit," David said.

Right on cue. "What is it?"

"I'm sending Bert's note over to John now."

"Okay."

"Bob, you better put your arm out here and catch this thing," I said.

"Okay. There. We'll have a love letter in a second."

"What more do we need? A bottle of wine," I said.

"Got it," he said. "Good shot, John."

And the note was in our cell. Bob stashed his long line around the top of the hot water pipe, between the ceiling and the binder. To do that he was standing on the window ledge and holding on to the bars like a monkey. I turned out the light while he climbed. Then we filled the community cup with hot steaming water from the tap, sat cross-legged on our beds, made our coffee in the small cups, lit our Camels, sat back, and puffed smoke at each other.

"That's the secret of an English education," I said.

"What's that?" he asked.

"They smoke at each other. The tutor and the scholar. Sit over wine and papers in the tutor's digs and smoke at each other."

Bob was reading the note. I quietly enjoyed my coffee and relished the Camel. Such sweet cemented limitation.

"Your turn," he said, handing me the letter. "We better turn the light off after you finish."

And I read the penciled letter in its tortured adolescent hand. Hands. Both wrote, one to a side. Such a down. No wonder no one has anything to say. Not even Bob. Where were we? he asks. Why didn't they, the men on the front lines of resistance, receive our support? Why don't we admit that we're copping out? We should be doing what they're doing: not working, not shaving, fasting sometimes, messing up count. We should be in the "hole," not Allenwood. Why don't we admit to failure, to unheroic activity, to ungenerous involvement.

All that movement jazz. Rhetoric. Like putting on armor. Such a down. No wonder I didn't want to read this convoluted squared-off message. It's too much. I looked at Bob. He's going to find some good in it to be cheerful about, I'll bet my last Camel on it. One keeps a brother, but one does not pamper him. Does no good to hide reality from them. No good to remain hidden as they are in their own fantasy-world. Love letter. Parcel Posted Psyche Rape. Have some coffee.

"Okay to turn off the light now?" Bob asked.

"Yes, let it go out."

Better watch out or all this sweet cemented limitation will turn into mud. This coffee into turpentine. He referred to the walk as a prank. Not serious revolutionaries. Damn, we're not in here on a whim. It is not chance that got us here. It does no good to hurl such doubt into these cells. How can they say we failed them? Failed them? We did not know about them. There were so many other things. They were but a segment of a scene in the corner of a sketch of the microcosm we were confronting. And Bert says we failed. Who are they in all the world, after all? Two fucked up blown minds who found Revolution and Peace Movement and Love and Community. Household idols in hippie drag. Yes, idols for you, too. But I've stuffed them differently. What right have they to impose their neuroses on us? Have we not our own?

"How about sharing a George?" Bob asked.

"We still have the Camels, don't we?"

"Yes, but I thought we could do a George and then finish up with a Camel."

"Gloomy in here," I said.

"Hack's coming," I heard David yell. We tossed our cigarettes into the toilet and flushed them away. Finished off the coffee and put the cups out of sight. The hack came by, stuck his flashlight up to the bars, and illuminated our cell briefly. Then he passed on to the next cell.

The Hole / 152

"A gloomy fucking cell, I say. A bloody pit." The hack left the block.

"Shall we light a George?" Bob asked.

"Why not."

"Why don't you write something to Bert and Rich?" he asked.

"What am I to say?"

"Say what you feel."

"That I think they're arrested adolescents playing cowboys and Indians with Hendricks and Rauch, whom they love more than hate?"

"Be a little more tactful than that," Bob said.

"Yes, one must not show one's 'impeccable rectitude,' as Dick says."

"Anyway, I think you should write them something."

"Okay, tomorrow I'll write something."

He handed me the smoldering butt of a George.

"This stuff would burn better in a fireplace," I said.

"Pretty bad," he said.

I got up and walked back and forth in the cell. Then I stood in the doorway, put my palms on the casement above me, and stretched. It felt damp. Cold. I was able then to strain with all my force. The corridor seemed lifeless and dull. Not much going on this evening. I went back to the mattress and had another pull on the George.

"We'll light the Camels from this. Save the pieces for tomorrow," Bob said. "Can't find them in the dark, anyway."

I went back to the door. It was something anyway to exert all my energy on that casement. Samson at least had Delilah. We've got Bert and Rich. The pieces. Yes, in the dark. Two matches apiece. Two and two do not make four. Dostoevsky was right. Two and two makes eight or more.

"Were Ernest here I'd tell him all about it," I said to no one in particular.

"All about what?" Bob asked.

"Men Without Women," I said.

"What would you tell him?" he asked.

"That it's a bore. A crashing drag."

The Hole / 153

"Come on, we'll have our Camels and hit the sack."

"So fucking good this Camel."

"I'm getting a little dizzy. Are you?"

"Yes, it's nice. Soft and gentle smoke."

But the cigarette did not last. The anger returned. I was not tired. In fact, I was terribly awake. The coffee. Bob was stretched out, his blanket over him. The spotlight flashed briefly on the wall and sidled out the window. Their bloody love letter. And I must write something for them tomorrow. What can I write? That won't hurt. Failed them. Wants us to comment on their thing. No mention of the hunger strike. Keeping Chandler out of the nut-house. I suppose we failed then, too?

I have written for them. That Friar Tuck piece. That was a delicious bit, that pseudonym. Dick and Mary's name for me. Fit in well. How did I put it in that essay— Oh, yes, "As for myself, Friar Tuck, I am but the spirit of a maverick monk, who has heard of these happenings, involving men now sequestered in the Sherwood Forests and gaols of contemporary America." Should change "sequestered"—little heavy. So was Tuck. Too bad it never got published. Had it all set up. A week to write it, another week before deadline. Had it kited out in time—all sixteen handwritten pages—the whole manuscript kited out all but in front of the hack's eyes. Not very bright. And then the fuck up. Didn't know where to send it. As if I wrote for anything but the *Worker*. So what if it's like scribbling on a gravestone. I'm still an editor of it, aren't I?

But I wrote it. For them, too. Finish off the little action inside with something that might get attention and more support outside. Wasn't a failure, anyway. Chandler wouldn't be down there now telling us we failed if we hadn't done that whole bit. He'd be drugged and lobotomized by now. Springfield.

How am I to sleep with this head? Wish I had my pipe. Bob's all curled up. Facing the wall. Why not do the essay? All of it? It'll come back once you're into it. That first part about Herr Reiger the Shrink is rich. Say so myself. Why not? Pass the time. Keep my anger down. Okay. The title:

The Hole / 154

The Springfield Solution:
Or How Not To Cope with Noncooperators

by Friar Tuck

And then that quote from Laing:

Psychiatry could be, and some psychiatrists are, on the side of
transcendence, of genuine freedom, and of true human growth.
But psychiatry can so easily be a technique of brainwashing, of
inducing behavior that is adjusted, by (preferably) non-in-
jurious torture. In the best places, where straitjackets are
abolished, doors are unlocked, leucotomies largely forgone, these
can be replaced by more subtle lobotomies and tranquillizers
that place the bars of Bedlam and the locked doors *inside* the
patient.

—*R. D. Laing*

And then the beginning. See how far you can go. Three parts
—remember:

1

In vain did he put his best face forward. The Chief Psychiatrist for the Federal Bureau of Prisons, stationed at the Federal
Penitentiary at Lewisburg, Pennsylvania, Dr. Wolfgang Reiger,
a tall, ruggedly handsome man with a shock of thin blond hair,
could not hide his anxiety behind his now open features and
nervous smile.

Had we all met in some quaint inn in the Alps, perhaps we
would have lifted high mugs of ale. But cornered as we were,
we political prisoners in cast-off Army khaki, he in an elegant
black uniform with gold braid and stripes, together with the
Superintendent of Allenwood Prison Camp, Mr. R. R. Engle (a
small man who tends to stand when others sit), all hurriedly met
and all but knee to knee in the latter's narrow office, this
"shrink," as he good-naturedly referred to himself, was hard put
to sell himself to us.

When we had entered that office, habitually in line and as if into a cage, we were met by his eager, extended hand and greeted with the title "Mister." I looked around for whom he was addressing: so strange was that title to my ears, attuned as they have been these long months only to my last name and number. I found myself muttering, "I am, I suppose, *Mister* Tuck," and tried to contain my laughter. He soon had our attention fixed: as much by his earnestness as by his thick (but, in one so young, charming) German accent. Each of us felt that at last here was a prison official who respected our image of ourselves. We were being liked, and being liked seemed to impose the duty of liking in return.

"I do not want to be known as, and I want to dispel any illusion you might have that I am," he said once we were all seated, "one of those bureaucrats, such as they have in foreign countries, who send political prisoners to insane asylums to have their minds *blitzed.*"

Although the sense of his statement is accurately presented here, I may not have all his words or his structure exactly: I was still beguiled by his German accent and a little intimidated and amused by the black of his uniform. Along with his anxiety that his speech and uniform might be detrimental to his argument, he conveyed his sense of being hurt that we should even *think* ill of him. He was a friend, he said smilingly, of our friends David and Kathy Miller; and he was as opposed to the war in Vietnam as we were. He spoke our language: that is, he used with familiarity and ease such slang words as "shrink," "copout," "run down," "rap," etc. He appealed to the absent number of prisoners who would testify to his being a "good guy." His young, handsome face obviously wanted to be loved; and his openness with, and respect for, us seemed to leave us little room and less reason for any expression of animosity. He seemed to imply that we were betraying him. Surely the classical art of rhetoric is still being taught in Germany.

Having stolen our thunder with his remark about not intending to blitz the minds of political prisoners, he went on to say he had come to "run down straight" to us, from his official records, his evaluation of Richard Chandler, a noncooperating C.O. at Lewisburg, and why he recommended that Chandler be

The Hole / 156

sent to the Springfield Federal Institution in Illinois, where he would be under the care of a psychiatrist. Also, he had heard from inmates at the "Wall" (Lewisburg prison) that some of us at Allenwood were on a hunger strike in protest over that transfer. More likely, he had heard of the strike from Associate Warden Hendricks and Captain Ryan, with whom three of us had conferred earlier this day in an unusual or unsuccessful attempt to see Chandler in the Wall. Perhaps on this day, February 18, 1970, he had passed on his way from Lewisburg to Allenwood the picket lines of student protesters from Bucknell University's and Philadelphia's Resistance groups, led by Richard Drinnon, Professor of History at Bucknell and author of the definitive biography of Emma Goldman, *Rebel in Paradise*.

Anyway, he wanted to dissuade us from such an action and was much pleased with his main argument against it, viz., that Mr. Hendricks' stomach did not bother him in the least. But he was primarily concerned with convincing us that he had Chandler's best interests in mind in recommending him to Springfield. Wasn't he, Dr. Reiger, the one who had secured for Chandler a two-year reduction in sentence? Surely he was and he did; no one denies that. Of course, he did that earlier in Chandler's confinement and at a time when he had had a rapport with Chandler. He confessed to having no longer that rapport, and that that was his primary reason for recommending his transfer.

That's all of Part 1. Easy. Reiger. Strange dude. Forgot to mention that he was working in a prison rather than Vietnam. Same as the dentists downstairs. Major point. Tony screamed at him in the office. Couldn't write about that. Or that first meeting. Bert came to my cube and asked me to come in on it. Knew what it would mean. Knew where his head was. He couldn't take Allenwood. Couldn't relate to guys. Knew Chandler was lonely in segregation by himself. They almost offed Bert over the record room. Wanted to get back into the "hole." In here where he could keep it at a distance. That meeting. In the reading room. Tony and Bud going to stop work. Bad vibrations.

The Hole / 157

Had to talk them out of it. No good. Your stopping work doesn't stop the works. No effect. Need pressure, inside and outside. Get Dick to set up picket lines here and at Lewisburg. Do a hunger strike. We don't want to be busted. No use then. But they wanted so to be busted. Take attention away from Chandler. Tony was pissed. Bud, too. But we got it started. Second Part was about Chandler and his thing. Should give that to him. Try it.

2

Noncooperators, such as Richard Chandler, who have the ability to say "No" at will to every regulation, command, and common procedure within a prison; and the grit to endure the punishments that necessarily ensue: prolonged segregation, the "hole," the "strip cell," harassment, and beatings; and the stamina to continue fasting, going limp when handled, take revocation of "good time" and threats of additional time and violence—such men pose special problems to everyone concerned within and without the prison system.

Prison administrators deal swiftly with prisoners who refuse to work; but political prisoners who refuse to work are not speedily taken to court, convicted, given additional time, etc. They are usually put in segregation for a few weeks and then released to their former work. The noncooperator thus poses for the administrator a threat to his impartiality, his fairness in dispensing punishment. The administrator must mete out what he considers justice fairly to all prisoners, if he is to retain the respect of his staff and gain the reputation of being a "fair" man with the inmates.

Mr. Hendricks, the Associate Warden of Lewisburg, who has the reputation of being a "fair" man, in speaking of Chandler and his prolonged (some thirteen months) noncooperation, referred to his relationship with him as one of "adoption." He felt he had "gone along," tolerated Chandler long enough. He allowed him to keep his hair long, his beard unshaved; he had promised that if Chandler would agree to go to Allenwood, he, Mr. Hendricks, would so arrange. Much to his credit, Mr. Hendricks honestly admitted that Chandler was "violently opposed" to the transfer to Springfield. But he was tired of Chandler's absolutism: when a guard would have to "butt" (read: function as a butler) to Chandler: i.e., retrieve the tray of dishes from his cell because Chandler refused to cooperate by pushing the tray out of his cell himself, then Mr. Hendricks commented that "Chandler isn't 'man' enough to do that much." In the eyes of his staff, he went on, he was a fool for putting up with Chandler.

Of course, the element of "saving face" is important here, for the privilege system is so pervasive within the prison that all claims to impartiality are pure rhetoric anyway. What is evident, also, in Mr. Hendricks' self-righteous remark is the prevailing institutional notion of human nature. As Irving Goffman says in *Asylums*, "The translation of inmate behavior into moralistic terms suited to the institution's avowed perspective will necessarily contain some broad pre-suppositions as to the character of human beings." "C.O.'s," as we are commonly called, have not ranked very high in their estimation; although, as will be seen, a change in that view may be evident.

Goffman also sheds some light on Dr. Reiger's predicament:

> Although there is a psychiatric view of mental disorder and an environmental view of crime and counter revolutionary activity, both forcing the offender from moral responsibility for his offense, total institutions can little afford this particular kind of determinism. Inmates must be caused to *self-direct themselves* in a manageable way. (p. 86.)

Political prisoners who refuse to "self-direct" themselves on principle may not appear to be the problem of a psychiatrist. Yet in Chandler's case the psychiatrist has played an essential role. As a tool of the administrative arm, a psychiatrist's recommendation could be a slick way of handling troublesome political prisoners, just as it has been effective in dealing with "hard ass" cons and other "maladjusters to the institution," to use the psychiatric label.

Dr. Reiger's primary reason, as stated before, for recommending Chandler's transfer was his lack of rapport with the inmate.

The Hole / 159

On the level of professional ethics, this response may appear dubious. Lack of rapport is a double-edged phenomenon, cause for it being found in the psychiatrist as well as the patient. Such a lack does not seem to warrant a transfer (the axe) as much as another, or possibly none at all, psychiatrist. Alas, we were told by the man himself that there are no other "Dr. Reigers."

But Dr. Reiger is not simply a psychiatrist; he is a psychiatrist in a federal prison: one of a number of high officials responsible for the easy sailing of this ship of convicts through the white waters of Time. As such, he is vulnerable to pressure exerted from nonmedical sources, i.e., the Warden and Associate Warden. His role, as well as the Chaplain's, embraces that of "mediator" or "troubleshooter" between the administration and inmates. Hence the need to have rapport with all groups, being a good guy, and his hurried conference with us; but given pressing priorities, he must be able to work under pressure. It would appear that he works well under pressure.

Noncooperators also pose a special problem to the other political prisoners. And here the term "political prisoners" should be clarified, for while it serves well as a blanket to cover Selective Service violators of the non-Jehovah's Witness, non-Amish varieties, it is nonetheless inaccurate if applied to those remaining. "Political" can hardly be a term applied to that mixed bag of shattered psyches. The Black Muslims would not, on their own, be classed with us, even though they are more politically here than we are. Nor does the term "resisters" suffice. Some are actually here by mistake, theirs or the court's. Some consider all prisoners political prisoners and hence refuse the label. Thus we C.O.'s are all frustratingly unique, hampered by own luggage and possessed of only the small arms of our souls for protection during our own confinement.

To individual forms of action such as Chandler's, a common response is that he's doing his own thing. We respect it; it isn't ours; but "Good luck." We who have opted for functioning, in one way or another, within the system view the absolute position as one we might be capable of if pushed to the wall; but if let alone to do our time, it seems unnecessary and unrealistic. Absolutism can be carried too far, this view maintains, and noncooperation with the system becomes noncooperation with life itself.

We know the counterargument as well: that to live or work, even to eat or shit within a prison, implies a tacit acceptance of the institution's right to confine us. To function at all, other than keeping one's mind and integrity intact, is a form of cooperation. And we all cooperate—orderlies, kitchen staff, teachers, librarians, cattle and farm crews. We all help the bloody machine roll on. Teachers may rationalize that they directly help men, not the institution; but, obviously, they help the institution's fictional program of rehabilitation. Even the hardest working of prisoners, the cattle crew, have the decided advantages of being away from the compound and "bitch box," active in the most human work of caring for cattle, and have the pleasure of friends around whom to work. We, along with every other prisoner, have our own little hustles going, have made primary and secondary adjustments, and are reluctant to do more "hard time" than we have already done.

In short, a day in our life is most unlike a day in the life of Ivan Denisovich, as Solzhenitsyn records it. His day was challenging, for he faced elementary struggles against hunger, exposure, psychic and physical annihilation. We face no such threat. If anything is threatened, once we are in our ruts, it is the peace of mind of born and bred middle-class children in a middle-class prison camp. In such a frame of mind one can get more upset over the lack of a reading light in his cubicle than over the transfer of Chandler.

But if we were content, during the past year, to do our time as Chandler was doing his in segregation, the news of his being transferred to Springfield shocked us into action. Noncooperation within a prison is admirable, if one can handle it; noncooperation in a mental hospital is a matter of being handled, with drugs and a host of other twentieth century torture methods. Noncooperation at Springfield would be predictably diagnosed as regression, prison psychosis, or acute depersonalization.

Springfield is not one of those "best places" mentioned by R. D. Laing, previously quoted. I have known prisoners, severely altered in personality and natural energy, who have been there; and many others who have friends who were sent there. "Shock treatments" and lobotomies are still commonly practiced there on the "criminally insane." As one prisoner put it, "God, you can't believe it. They play ping-pong without the ball."

Wouldn't change it. A little propagandistic. Nothing that simple. The doc said he'd go along with the hunger bit if Chandler hadn't had a psychiatric history. Been to shrinks before. The doc was okay. Played that role to the hilt. Big powerful man. Had beautiful daughter, wife. Hung out too much with that religious rat. But he came into the cube and said he would have gone along, not because he believed in what we believed in. He was a Navy man. Said he respected me. Knew we were trying to help. Told him it didn't disprove anything for me if Chandler had prior shrink experience. Damn few haven't. Even if Chandler was hiding, so to speak, behind leftist rhetoric, "noncooperation," in an effort not to be exposed to population because of that horror show he went through in the D.C. county jail—that didn't alter the fact that he's sane, as Reiger says, and not fodder for the Springfield place. Even if that were so, at least he's got his head and emotions together around something. Psychological roots to our political stances. Trees are not trees only from the ground up.

Psychic rape, that letter though. Roots to the psyche. What was it Laing wrote? Personal worlds rediscovered are a shambles. Something like that. The other part. Well put. Bodies half-dead; genitals dissociated from heart; heart cut off from head; head cut off from heart. Something like that. Without inner unity, with just enough sense of continuity to clutch at identity. Yes, or an ideology full of rhetoric. Identity there, too. What was the rest? Something about man being cut off from his own mind, cut off equally from his body—"a half-crazed creature in a mad world." That's it. Half-crazed—not simply that. That compounded by as many selves as we have cells almost. Each half-crazed when strung out.

Well, Chandler's together around something. Whatever it is is to be respected. That it poses a problem to Hendricks is suf-

The Hole / 162

ficient justification for it. The "fair" man. Heard him called so by Mafia types, Jimmy for example. In their case, probably so. He needs to make concessions to them, work smoothly with them, deal with them as if in his eyes they were men. Has to keep his ship sailing. They control a damn good part of it, too. All to the good. But they shouldn't be so easily led along. He uses them as much as they use him. But he has no use for C.O.'s. They are not a power within the Wall. Out at Allenwood, maybe. Here, they're a problem. Too articulate, too many friends higher up, too much support outside. Too keen on making his little shop known on the outside. It doesn't pay to be fair with them. And his bloody hacks can't hack it. Not sophisticated. "To butt" indeed. That's exactly what they are anyway. Servants. I can see them getting uptight about having to come in and get a tray. Must irk them just to do the feeding.

Just like him to use Reiger. Pass the buck. Under your authority, Doctor, on your recommendation, we'll send him to Springfield. Reiger's so obliging, too. So needs his image bolstered. How does he keep tabs on them all? Said in that meeting he'd been through analysis. Good for everyone, he says. Certainly it gave him a grip on all his hats.

How can he state that because he lacked a rapport with Chandler he feels Chandler should be transferred? What kind of mind is that? Relates Chandler to himself so completely. If Chandler balks, it's Chandler who's sick, not Reiger. Strange. Myopic view of things. Can't he see the jail he's working in? Isn't that a part of Chandler's experience? What was it he and the other shrink decided? Sane except for slight deterioration due to confinement. Slight deterioration, indeed. He's so busy being Reiger, being Reiger relating to Chandler, that he can't see Chandler as Chandler, Chandler as inmate, Chandler experiencing the "hole," experiencing Reiger. Takes care of his own house, that's all it amounts to. If his house has an uncooperative guest, get rid of him. Good housewife. Sweeps dirt under rugs, hangs bed linen out windows.

If he were real in his role, he wouldn't allow himself to be used so by Hendricks. Real? How real is his role? Such a role precludes an ethic. So what ethic can he carry into it? All the

The Hole / 163

knowledge and training at his command. Yields what? Bigger and better ways to imprison men effectively. Great service there. Help them adjust to castration, confinement, futility, despair, and death. Keep up the good work, Doctor. You're a good tool. Handyman. Fix up this psyche, Doc. He refuses to eat for no reason, refuses to work. Can't have that, Doc. Got anything to help him? Pills, drugs, a little strip cell all by himself for a while? A little water poured on him to remind him we're still thinking of him?

Such is psychiatry in the service of governments, not science, much less truth. I wonder if he ever thinks about it? At night, before shutting off the light on his role, his uniform, his faces, does he brood upon what he causes, what changes such power can effect in men? Can he really believe he is doing good? Must. "I'm the only Dr. Reiger," or something like that, he said. But that was a face. One shown in public, but not to his peers. When the light is out, what does he say? To which self, I wonder?

Chandler is indeed a problem. To us, too. To me. Why can't I buy that scene? No joy in it, I think. I'd rather walk once as we did than refuse to eat a thousand times. Can't noncooperate with life itself. That's to noncooperate with what one is trying, after all, to affirm. Yes, in the face of its constant and repeated denial. Anarchist's Folly. I swear it is better to walk over the hill joyfully, to carry the misery out, to leave the drudgery behind, to join with others in freedom—even if it leads into the "hole." Best, if it does of a certainty lead to the "hole." Rather than inflict upon others a self-imposed martyrdom that but reminds them of their own suffering. Confront the system with a little grace. Confront it humanly. As humanly as possible, not as inhumanly as they make you, as they force you to become. With others. Never alone. That's to invite evaporation and melting at the same time. So snow banks disappear under high winds and higher temperatures. From the top and from the bottom. Unless with friends and for friends and with vicariously as many as one can handle. Infectious, too. Catches on. Good for the guys in the camp. That's why fasting is such a violent thing. Can't be shared really. Makes everyone else an "other" than you. All that's communicated is intimidation and rage. Intimidation and rage at them by you; at themselves by themselves because of you.

Yes, but there was Olaf and now there's Chandler. But even he: "I sing of Olaf/Glad and big." Cummings has him "glad and big." Yes, "There is some shit I will not eat/I will not kiss your fucking flag." Articulate, old Olaf was. Paid for it, too. We get off a little scarred, that's all. He was gentle, too.

"To individual forms of action such as Chandler's, a common response is that he's doing his own thing." Yes, I said that as gently as I could. It's not in doing one's own thing that anything is achieved. It's in doing another's thing because he can't do it or won't or is too hung up to do it. Picking up the burdens of others. That cup of water. Flow together. Needs someone to be at the center. Someone stronger than I certainly. My psyche is not consistent enough. Too many ups and too many crashing downs. Had to do it. No one else was there. And it had to be done. And look at the group in here. So beautiful. In the shower room. Give a name to that if you can. Brotherhood and Fellowship—too large, too cold in a way. The Shape of Love. No ideological bonds; no need, in the end, for fife, drum, and flag. As natural as an earthen bowl. How they blossomed. David hopping in the field, John's stately march. It all came out. What was intrinsically beautiful in each blossomed in that field. Beauty chased by angry pigs, uniformed boars. On the way to the crest of the hill. Too much.

Still can't sleep. This churning mind will give me no rest. Like that spotlight. In and out. Should time it. To hell with it. See how it sidles into the cell. Finds a bare wall. Can't go any further. Then it must retreat. As if it were crawling backwards. Hits the corner and moves sideways. Hits the window, finds an opening, and flows stealthily outside. Even got light behaving like a criminal. Have to keep my head together in this place. It is so fucking destructive of sense and meaning.

It is time to do the third and final part of the essay. Can't leave it incomplete. It's about the use of your insane asylums. So shine again, spotlight. The third act of our little play will be performed for you. Shine on.

The Hole / 165

Extenuating circumstances, however, within the prison at Lewisburg, severely alter the whole picture of Chandler's transfer as it has been thus far sketched. What became apparent in repeated conferences with prison officials was the real threat to Chandler's safety in segregation. That threat came from guards, who were in a highly "uptight" frame of mind because of the riot that occurred in January 1970 in Lewisburg, which hospitalized twenty guards, some seriously, one remaining on the critical list. No inmates were hurt. Recently augmented by eight, the guards now working in Lewisburg, especially in segregation where some of the alleged rioters are confined, are angry, bitter, frightened, and quick to violence. It is reported that some guards now carry clubs or blackjacks. The atmosphere of the prison, as recent visitors and inmates from Allenwood can testify, is very "tight" and explosive.

Seen in this light, Mr. Hendricks' insistence on Chandler's transfer out of segregation, and Dr. Reiger's supportive response, are truly humanitarian gestures, albeit somewhat desperate ones and not primarily in Chandler's best interest. One wonders whether the psyches of guards or that of a prisoner is the main concern here.

When we first learned of Chandler's pending transfer on Friday, February 13, from Ralph Bertolucci, a nonresister but close friend of Chandler's who had been to the Wall, two resisters here immediately presented themselves to the Superintendent and requested an interview with Mr. Hendricks in hopes of securing one with Chandler. Mr. Hendricks at first indicated Saturday as the day for his interview, changed it to Monday evening, and on Monday evening we were told he was unavoidably detained and would be in to see us on Tuesday.

By Sunday evening, however, we had decided on our tack. Work stoppage was argued down because it was absurd to call a work stoppage and have the works go on; also, it would lead to an immediate bust. Our primary concern was to delay Chandler's transfer, which was scheduled for early the coming week. To be busted would take us out of the picture. Inside and outside pressures were needed. Obviously, it was our ability to

It was reported, however, that their first encounter was with Captain Ryan, who would negotiate the meeting with Chandler. His office is carpeted and richly paneled, with black leather chairs and draperies. Upon entering he was reported to be sitting behind his desk, his back to the far corner of the room. Although these resisters have entered many offices of officials in their time, it was noted that never was there so clearly an atmosphere of climbing into a boxing ring and finding one's heavyweight opponent in the opposite corner as there was on this occasion. Captain Ryan inspires fear. It turned out that Chandler would not promise the administration that he would return voluntarily to his cell after the meeting. In view of the likelihood of guards having to handle him in such a situation, the visit was denied.

On their way to Receiving and Delivery, where they would have to wait for the return trip to Allenwood, the three envoys were called back and told that Mr. Hendricks wished to see them. Captain Ryan, who was unsuccessful in his earlier attempts to measure the concern of these men, was also present at this time but silent, somewhat in the manner of a time bomb. Mr. Hendricks, on the other hand, was reported to be in a more gracious mood; he was sincerely unhappy at the impossibility of their visiting Chandler and indicated that authorization for the transfer to Chandler had not yet arrived from Washington. No mention of a hunger strike or pickets was made by either party, although somehow the presence of these realities was felt. He congratulated the resisters, upon their leaving, for the "grand effort" they made on Chandler's behalf.

Upon their return to Allenwood, Ralph Bertolucci, upset by the aborted visit to Chandler, rashly and without warning requested to be sent to segregation to be with his friend. Mr. Engle said he would let him know. The next day Bertolucci was transferred to the Wall.

Following this unexpected action was the equally unexpected visit of Dr. Reiger, already partially narrated. It should be emphasized that Dr. Reiger, in reading from his reports, noted that neither he nor an outside psychiatrist, called in especially to collaborate with Reiger on Chandler, could affix to Chandler any psychiatric label. He is not, according to their own diagnoses, fill segregation, where Mr. Hendricks did not want even Chandler to be, that provided us with some needed leverage. So we decided on ye olde hunger strike as a delaying tactic. A hunger strike with some modifications, however: we would not make any statement of intent or issue any ultimatum to any administration about the strike; instead we would have it announced by rumor inside and by pickets and the local news media outside, thereby saving us from a political act that would entail a direct response from officials. If questioned, only individual noneating, not that of a group, would be affirmed. No disruptive action was planned for the mess hall.

When Mr. Hendricks arrived on Tuesday, none of this action was made known to him, although during the discussion he complained of bad vibrations and veiled threats. His line at this time was strong: Chandler would definitely be transferred; any confrontation we sought would be speedily dealt with in segregation, where he insisted he had plenty of room. He generously agreed to permit three of us to travel to Lewisburg in an effort to see Chandler. And further agreed that no action against Chandler would be taken until we had conferred with Chandler, if possible, and with him, Mr. Hendricks, afterward. That highly unusual meeting was set up for Wednesday morning.

By this time, however, sympathizers on the outside, in Lewisburg and Philadelphia, had become aware of the situation. Chandler's family, lawyers (injunction in pocket), sympathetic congressmen and senators, and, of course, the news media, were being notified. Much of the work of the outside supporters remains unknown to us, and one remains in the somewhat absurd position of peering into a microscope and seeing only one's own eye. Our response to such solidarity is truly felt if not adequately expressed.

The trip that Wednesday of three political prisoners from Allenwood to Lewisburg must for the most part remain in darkness. Too detailed a description might bring unwanted heat on the participants. (As for myself, Friar Tuck, I am but the spirit of a maverick monk, who has heard of these happenings, involving men now sequestered in the Sherwood Forests and gaols of contemporary America.)

The Hole / 167

mentally ill in any certifiable sense. They did affirm that he had a rigid personality, was morally and ethically oriented, and, if anything, could be described as an autistic type, i.e., more concerned with himself than with others. Dr. Reiger also mentioned the obvious: that Chandler was not happy in segregation, but he concluded this was due to his psyche, not the circumstances. Again, his formal cause for recommending Chandler's transfer was his lack of a rapport; and we have noted what we believe to be the efficient cause—the pressure of high officials for the expedient removal of a possibly embarrassing and painful case.

In the face of opposition from the political prisoners, Dr. Reiger, at the end of the session, agreed to try to find another prison to which Chandler might be transferred: one "hole" being similar to any other "hole" but dissimilar to Springfield's accommodations. The worst that Lewisburg could offer a prisoner, we were quite ready to believe, might be better than the best Springfield would offer a mental patient. He promised to call the next day, but no call was forthcoming.

On Thursday and Friday, local newspapers were carrying the story and regional and state news were bringing it over the TV into the camp. Other forms of outside pressure were also being exerted. Larry and V. Scott and George Willoughby, longtime activists in the Peace Movement and friends of one resister, tried unsuccessfully to meet with Chandler and later, with Mr. Hendricks, met with the resisters at Allenwood.

Inside we were faced with the problem of what to do after the smoke cleared; Mr. Hendricks would still be in a position to transfer Chandler once the clamor ended. To circumvent this possibility we drafted the following message to Mr. Hendricks:

We earnestly request to be transferred to Lewisburg's "hole" on the very day you transfer Chandler to Springfield; or on any day prior to that time should that transfer be non-negotiable.

Rather than sign and submit our trump card, we permitted it to be announced by the local news media. We were still left with a hunger strike that could not go on indefinitely, for the cattle and farm crews had to do physical labor. We were substantially assisted, it should be noted, by regular cons, who provided high protein honey and other high protein additives for use in coffee or hot chocolate.

A bizarre demonstration was suggested, received enthusiastically and might have been effective in many ways. In the unventilated, smoke-filled room where we met, everyone's handkerchief was out and up to his eyes, whether from smoke, rage, or glee remains unknown. Enthusiasm waned, however, for the little venture; it did entail some risk, but is so delightful it should not be thrown away.

Taking a more than myopic look at the situation, we realized that it was the conditions within an uptight prison that should be made known, not simply the predicament of one Selective Service violator. If we could bring attention to bear on the repressive conditions all prisoners face, we might do some substantial good. Especially since, owing to the riot of Black Muslims, the surrounding community was less than sympathetic to prisoners, especially Black prisoners.

And so it happened that on Tuesday, February 24, over half the population of Allenwood Prison Camp—Blacks, Whites, Puerto Ricans, hard-core cons, and just plain victims—joined the political prisoners in boycotting the noon meal. Thus our strike went out with a bang. No disruptive action was needed. It was simply a matter of staying away from the Polish sausage that (happily) was being served in the mess hall. Mr. Engle and Mr. McInnes, who is in charge of the kitchen, were faced with a rather empty hall and full pans of sausage. We regret Mr. McInnes' reported anger and thank him for the plentiful fresh milk and good meals he served after the strike concluded.

All prisoners are more or less aware of "Springfield," know or have heard of the "vegetables" it creates, dislike the widespread use by prison officials of arbitrary transfer, and are sympathetic to a group of men who stand up for one of their own. We believe that this sympathy boycott on behalf of a "C.O." by over 175 other prisoners makes a new relationship possible between political prisoners and others of various races, ethnic backgrounds, and political viewpoints. "We are all convicts, first," was the striking response. No longer are we so readily labeled "kooks" and ostracized. They know what we can do, and that we are not interested only in "C.O.'s."

On this Tuesday, supporting picket lines at the Federal Courthouse in Lewisburg, at the penitentiary, and at Allenwood appeared along with the press. Other demonstrations, organized by the Philadelphia Resistance Group, were staged in Philly and, it is rumored, at other Federal prisons.

And for the sake of the local community, prison officials, students of Bucknell, and us, Richard Drinnon was holding class out in the street again, talking to newspapermen and relating this small issue to the conviction and sentencing of the Chicago 8, which was happening at the same time. Neither official Washington nor the Silent Majority should be allowed to believe that by imprisoning dissenters they have succeeded in silencing them.

Pedagogically, it is always good to have an example of repression in one's own back yard. And this particular form of repression, the Springfield solution for noncooperating C.O.'s, must be challenged on every level possible. With our wits about us, the future indeed seems bleak and desperate. What would it be without any wits at all?

Political mind-blitzing may or may not be a potential threat to dissenters in this country. We know it has been a real threat to one draft resister, who went on to resist the prison system as well.

It was during the boycott of the noon meal that we first learned that Ralph Bertolucci had been into some difficulty after his transfer to the Wall. The rumor was that he had been beaten and maced. The next day we received confirming word from Bertolucci himself that he had been "kicked, maced, thrown, and drugged"; that he was a "mental patient" in Lewisburg's psycho ward; and that he wanted "Help!" He also is reported to have been tried before the "Kangaroo court" in Lewisburg as a leader of the Allenwood political prisoners: a rather cheap play, we think, considering Bertolucci the scapegoat walked into the

The Hole / 171

cage himself. But it must look good on official records, appease some staff, and take some people off the hook.

As of this writing, both Bertolucci and Chandler are in adjoining cells in Lewisburg's "hole." Chandler, according to Dr. Reiger, will not be transferred to Springfield. Dr. Reiger blames us, the political prisoners of Allenwood (trump card still in hand) for that and also for Chandler's missed opportunity to be happy at Springfield. We are flattered but not disarmed; we doubt there is much bliss in Springfield; and we accept the blame in the name of our outside supporters as well.

May we ever cooperate in solidarity with those who noncooperate in prison.

Did you enjoy the show, spotlight? You kept coming in and going out again as if you were displeased but fascinated. I should think you would be fascinated. Should I call upon Friar Tuck to annotate the performance? Fill in a few of the gaps? You return again. I take that as a request. But I feel I grow sleepy. It would be best to proceed with dispatch. Therefore we'll do it academically. Point by point, rather than ruminate. I think the Friar is up to that, but he's been in the green wood so long it is not likely to be as dry an affair as when he used to be in the priory. Good. Doing it academically will no doubt put me to sleep very quickly.

First of all, the Blacks. Or the Black Muslims rioting. Some of that human iron you crushed and piled in ghettos and jails. See how it acts when it winters in the head. When you confine behind gates and walls, when they can't even go out into the yard to exercise. And that limitation set upon them, the curtailment of their exercises, their personal expression for rage and hate, was at the root of that particular riot. The Black Muslims. All they want now is what you did not give them, what you yourself offered numerous times in the early years of this country, when slavery became an embarrassment and an economic drain—a place, a space to live away from Whitey, the Man. And now that they want it themselves, rather than simply what Whitey has that they've been denied, you refuse it to them. And they end up, along with so many other Blacks, in jail because that is the only space, the only place you've ever really provided for them.

Yes, and now those rioting Blacks are right down the block from me. Looking at forty or fifty years in jail, not the two or three they were sentenced to for draft refusal. You charge them with "mutiny" too. Is that a holdover from the slave ship syndrome?

Second, our tack. Seemed like so little to guys who wanted to be busted. But busted and who's to organize? So we used the picket lines, pressure from Peace people, the hunger strike. They were limited but effective. My weight lifting friends gave me honey and high protein food additives for the cattle crew and me. "Honey for the Red Bear." And they laughed when I told them of meeting that way with Ryan. Ryan is no laughing matter, though. So like a tiger hunting. Tense, wary, ready to spring and devour. Primed to kill. What a trip: Hendricks the Car Salesman; Rauch the Super-righteous Puritan; Ryan the Tiger.

Third, our press releases. Now there was little finesse, if I do say so. Some of my students on Work Release making phone calls to the news media and friends. And that bizarre demonstration would have been so good. A sit-in on top of the flat-roofed dormitory in full view of the control center, visitors, and, of course, the newspapermen, who would have been asked to arrive just as we sat down. Pull the ladder up after us. Let the wind carry leaflets to the visitors and newsmen. Of course, we'll come down immediately. Photographs already taken, message given. No problem. And it went over so well when first suggested. Glee in their eyes. John knew it would be good theater. But the next day they had second thoughts about hacks and inmates and violence on a rooftop. Small risk of that then, I thought. Still think.

Fourth, the boycott of the noon meal. So good. Tom and Mike got to the hard-core White, Tommy to the Italians, Nino to the Puerto Ricans, John and Nat to the Blacks. And that religious fink, rat mother fucker, who was following me around all that weekend, that final day. Smiling like a baby. What was it I said to him? He had followed me out on the back porch the

The Hole / 173

morning of the boycott. It was a bright sharp day. Snow and ice still in places. I stood and watched the sun over Penny Hill. The crows on the still black branches. He wanted so to talk to me. And I said nothing. Just drank my coffee as if he didn't exist. Then, seeing a strip of ice on the bank, he goes over to it and slides across it, slides back, slides again. A round, chubby rat sliding on ice. Too much. And he comes back to me with something to say.

."Gee, I wish I had a pair of ice skates," he said smilingly. "I'd go ice skating. Do you like to ice skate?" he asked sweetly.

"Have you ever tried skating on an administrator's heart?" I asked him without looking at him.

"Cold and hard?" he said innocently.

"Ice," I said, and left the porch.

Yes, and that stopped him for about an hour. But later when I was watching at the front window to see the guys who were and were not going up to the mess hall, there he was beside me. Winking he was, as if he knew about everything and was in on it. His almost bald head shining. He was butchered whenever he went to the barber's. How to skin a rat. Like they do to new-comers.

And the hunger strike was good. Some of the guys would go in, fill trays with dishes and bowls, go through the line without putting anything on them, get coffee, and sit down. The kitchen hacks just laughed the first few days. But it wore on them. They were not necessary to these noneating inmates. And they were angry. McKinnis angry as hell over the boycott. No one in the mess hall, all that food left over. Jerry counting the plates in the kitchen, so we knew how many stayed away.

And when I finally went into the mess hall. What a scene! Hadn't been near it for a week. Never showed my face. Did not want them to be able to say that all the strikers show up in the mess hall regularly. They know how to lie so well. Professionals at it. McKinnis was beaming as if he'd won at poker. And the fresh milk and fruit he put up that wasn't on the menu. The soft-boiled eggs that Nat got me. The welcome. It was fine, it was rich, it was good. McKinnis had his role back. He was needed. And the food, once I began to eat again, just made me feel heavy.

The Hole / 174

I came down with a crash. Could have fasted for another week. Felt that way, anyway.

Fifth, and let it be last. I will sleep I think. The political mind-blitzing. Reiger's own term. He knew what he was about. What the institution can so easily be programmed to do. Make use of the national resources, its institutions, to eliminate or control its natural resources, its people, land, and wealth. Bertolucci and Chandler. Truly, children of the bomb. Must write something for them tomorrow.

Take it on the hop, spotlight. Get out of my cell. The play is over. *Ite missa est.*

Thunder in the corridor resounding through our cell. We woke startled to look at each other.

"My God, that's louder than it was in the 'hole,'" I said to Bob.

"Yes," he said. "It sounds as if it came up all the way from the 'hole,' from the bowels of this place. Must be breakfast. Throw your mattress over on mine. We'll eat in my house today."

"Done," I said. "Do you always wake with imagery in your head?"

"What imagery?" Bob asked.

"Nothing," I said. "Here's our breakfast."

"You guys have a visit this morning," the hack said, giving us our trays of food. "I'll be back after we clean up breakfast."

"Who could be visiting us?" I asked Bob.

"Must be Joe Rogers. I'll check whether it's just us or all of us," and he went to the window and found out from the still sleepy voices that we all had a visit and we all had better be ready after breakfast. As if we could have gone for a stroll in the garden or something.

"Has to be Joe Rogers. Only the C.C.C.O. representative can visit all the C.O.'s," Bob said.

"Then we'll be seeing Phil Berrigan, too," I said.

"We should, yes."

"A good day, then," I said, and we ate our Sunday morning

The Hole / 175

spongy pancakes, coffee, and orange juice. The sun was brilliant in the cell.

"Would you care for a little poetry with your coffee?" I asked.

"Why not? Can you actually think so early in the morning?"

"I don't think so much as feel so early, but there are words for feeling as well as thinking, I guess. And once you've memorized a poem, it's always there in your psyche to put around a feeling."

"Okay," Bob said, "what's the poem?"

"It's called 'The Sun Rising' and it was written by John Donne, beautiful mystic and death-trip artist of the seventeenth century. I may not be able to get all the poem. I memorized it—must be ten or eleven years ago—as an undergraduate. I'm trying to get it together. Here it is, I think:

> Busy old fool, unruly sun,
> Why dost thou thus,
> Through windows, and through curtains call on us?
> Must to thy motions lovers' seasons run?
> Saucy pedantic wretch, go chide
> Late schoolboys, and sour prentices,
> Go tell court-huntsmen, that the King will ride,
> Call country-ants to harvest offices;
> Love, all alike, no season knows, nor clime,
> Nor hours, days, months, which are the rags of time.

"There's something missing I think from the beginning. I know 'rags of time'—what a phrase for it all!—ends it. Can't get the beginning."

"The sunlight in here made you think of that?" Bob asked.

"Yes, and the irony of it all. The poem's about two lovers waking up to the sun and Donne dismisses the sun in favor of his lover. So here we are, not lovers really, but at least in the same room, and waking to the sun, and I don't feel like dismissing the sun. Not that I have anything against you, Bob. I don't know whether love is all alike either. But Donne's into the old Platonic notion that love is timeless, etc. It's a cocky poem, I think. Dismissing the sun. As if one can't love in sunshine as well as darkness. I much prefer to see what I love anyway."

"You had to memorize poetry in college?" Bob asked.

"Yes, that's the other thing that reminded me of the poem. I memorized it for Dr. Loomis in a course in metaphysical poets. And Dr. Loomis, as well as one of my other profs then, Mr. McLean, were at the same time, the end of World War II, both Trappist monks in Gethsemane. They had what Mr. McLean called a three-year vocation. Seems like monasteries really fill up during and after a war. Gethsemane expanded all over, new monasteries founded. All GI's. Can you believe it? Into bread, cheese, and chant. Beautiful. So, anyway, they both leave the monastery and end up at the same college and meet in the hallway, embrace, and call each other by their monkish names. So beautiful they are. When I was expelled from that college—"

"You were expelled from college?"

"Oh, yes, you've never heard that story. Take a day to tell it all. So rich a trip in retrospect. But a horrow show at the time. I wrote a bad poem called, "A Humble Remonstrance to Intransigeant Authority" and was expelled for it in my senior year. Danforth Fellowship, Woodrow Wilson Fellowship candidate, etc. I won't tell it all. Anyway, when after all that went down and the decision was final, and the idiot-priest I wrote the poem about telling me that with glee in his eyes. Just another hack he was. Anyway, that night I take myself down to the dingy bars of Wilkes-Barre and proceed to get drunk. But students were following me. And they caught up with me and called Dr. Loomis, who came down to this crumby little bar and talked and talked and talked and I stopped drinking. Then he took me over to Mr. McLean's home where I stayed the night. The best part— the part I can't remember without cracking up—was the next morning. I'm going with Mr. McLean to mass. It's a weekday but he went to mass as many days of the week as many times a day as humanly possible. With finesse, too. With grace. So gentle and humble a man. So we go to mass. And I am still surging with anger. And the mass ends and Mr. McLean, so gently, suggests I go to confession so I can go to communion during the next mass. So rich. I didn't know whether to laugh or weep.

The Hole / 177

He wanted me to get rid of this anger that I grasped so tightly to my chest. And I couldn't refuse him. So up to the little dark box I go and do that thing. And out and back again to mass. And did that wafer thing, too, and returning, I assured myself in Jansenistic terms that truly here was the face of a gargoyle returning from communion. But it killed effectively my anger toward that red-haired priest who fucked me up. I just hate them in general now. Going to see Berrigan reminded me of those beautiful monk-teachers of mine."

"You were an active Catholic then," Bob asked.

"Yes, I was into the whole thing. But that experience sort of cured me of the institutional phase of the sickness called religion. That and the other thing—"

"What other thing?"

"Again, I don't want to go into it all. But you are looking at one of the few men of this century who have been ordered to leave the secular city by a clergyman. 'If you are not out of this city by Friday noon, your case will never be reconsidered.' That's what the President of that college told me. Too much. And, fool that I was, I left."

"Wasn't it a Dr. Loomis who visited you at Allenwood?" Bob asked.

"Yes, such a visit. To see this man with a wit centuries old and yet forever young in that visiting room just digging all the people there. At lunch we sat down to meat-loaf or something and I began without thinking to shovel the garbage down and he, without making me the least bit uncomfortable, says grace. Grace in a prison mess hall! That was a little much. Before I'll say grace over government food, I'll starve."

Thunder again in the corridor resounding through our cell.

"Why the hell," I asked, "is it so damned much louder up here than in the 'hole'? You've got the scientific mind, Bob, tell me. Up here we have windows open on the corridor and outside. I should think being so open a container the sound would be dissipated."

"I have no idea. But being shut up behind a solid iron door might have something to do with it. Must muffle some of the sound, keep it in the corridor and not in the cell."

The Hole / 178

"Our cells were opened and we all came together in the corridor. There was only one hack and he seemed a bit uptight. Laughing and rapping, we followed him down to the shower room.

"Looks like we get another shower," David said.

"Must be procedure. We don't need one," I said.

"Well, I can use one," he said, and we were off again on another glee-trip, compounded by anticipation over the visit.

But I was conscious of the uptightness of the hack as well as the fun and frolic of my friends. I wondered why he was alone, and I decided it must be because it was Sunday and fewer hacks would be on duty. He was impatient to get on to the next scene, a little out of touch with our circumstances. The last time we were in here the hack just took his time, gave us a full hour to play in. Not this guy. He was middle-aged and nervous. Thin lips tightly drawn. Horn-rimmed glasses, small bulging eyes. He can't stand waiting. Feels he's too busy to put up with clowning faggots. I'll bet that's what he's thinking. Got to do it all himself, too. He put a damper on my fun, but the others were just free-wheeling all around and obviously in no great hurry to get through the shower-and-shave scene.

"Finish up in there!" he said sharply. "I don't have all day. This isn't a hotel. Let's go!"

So we finished up. But his tenseness did not penetrate the glee and on our way down to the basement, through stairways and corridors and many locked doors, the glee was bubbling and flashing and hopping and rapping, and this uptight hack's neck was getting redder as his anger grew, until it became a very bright red as he fumbled with his keys and looked back at us infrequently, as if he were trying to control his anger. When we reached the basement, he turned and ordered us sharply to line up.

"Line up, here! In a row!" he shouted, as we made clumsy movements toward forming a line that would not quite resemble a line.

"Look here, you—" he broke in and anger was warring with frustration, "this visit is a privilege that I can put an end to right here. In line, I said!" And he turned quickly and led us

The Hole / 179

off in the direction of the clothing issue department.

I began to whistle. I whistled low and soft. And now that was the only sound besides our footsteps in the empty corridors, and we arrived at clothing issue where an inmate in pressed pants and starched shirt was waiting.

"Good you're here," the hack said to him. "Got to get these guys outfitted for a visit. If I had to wait on you, we'd be late."

"Came down as soon as I heard," the inmate said. "I've got their shorts, T-shirts, and socks all out. They'll need shoes, too, won't they?"

"Yeah, I've got the key to that, too. Okay, men, strip down and I'll shake you down before you put those things on."

He was relaxed now. Things were working out for him. He had time for all the procedures.

So we stripped again.

"Hands up. Open your mouth. Run your hands through your hair. Lift your balls. Turn around. Bend over. Spread those cheeks. Lift your feet. Okay. Next."

And we each submitted to this delightful little exhibition. Indians in a circle dance. Dickey was flashing all the while and the hack had to check his laughter. He was helpful now. He told the inmate to give us new blues. And he opened the shoe shop next door to the clothing issue door and gave us all the right size shoes we needed. He hunted up a comb for us and looked on as we gradually clothed ourselves and became presentable prisoners. "Handsome cons," as we told ourselves.

"You look like one of those 'gentle felons' that Dr. Gaylin wrote about in that book he called *In the Service of Their Country*," I said to David.

"That book about Dan and Steve? Is that the one?"

"Yeah, that unbook written by an unethical liberal for somewhat concerned liberals about the sad resisters, who are not really brave—it's just that they're fucked up and in need of Herr Gaylin's anachronistic analysis."

"If I ever meet him, I'll show him a 'gentle felon's' fist," David said.

"He dedicated it to the women in his life," I said.

"He doesn't deserve any," David said.

The Hole / 180

"Well, let's hope they can now measure their man against the men whose psyches he taped and then rushed to publish."

"What are you guys rapping about?" asked Jerry.

"Gaylin's book," David said.

"That creep."

"Are we ready, men?" said the hack in a quiet good-natured voice. He was about to pass us on to someone else and he would be on time.

"You ready, Hobbit?" David said.

"I'm fine. You ready, Jerry?"

"Grab the Hobbit, Davy," Jerry said.

And all at once I was up in the air, my legs making futile efforts to touch the floor as these two giddy cons, their arms under mine, carried me away.

"Hey, hey. This is no way for cons to behave," I said as I laughed suspended. They were striding away behind the hack as he led us past Jimmy Hoffa's now closed, unlit, and fenced-in mattress shop and out to the main door of the clothing exchange. And there I came down, partially, for I was still high.

"Let us go and make a visit," I said, in a tone inconsistent with the poem.

"Through half-deserted streets," John echoed.

"The muttering retreats," I said.

"Of—it isn't really appropiate," John concluded. "Though it is beautiful."

"True enough," I said. "His time was sadder than ours. And all he had left was imagination."

In the main corridor of the first floor, near the glassed-in control center (here the riot mentioned in the Friar Tuck piece had taken place), we were being eyed intensely, as we waited for doors to open, by other inmates, who must have wondered where these seven longhairs came from, how they got into new blues, and why if so new to the prison were they having a visit all together. Several of the men whistled. It was not all so comfortable a scene. For a moment I imagined doing the rest of my time in population here. That may be the verdict, I said to myself. But there wasn't time for much ruminating and no time for remorse. We were still moving as we seemed to have been

The Hole / 181

since breakfast. We were now in the narrow corridor where various officials of the prison, including the associate wardens, Rauch and Hendricks, had their offices. At the end of the corridor was a small room in which prisoners were stripped and searched before entering the visiting room on the other side.

Our hack went ahead of us and, after hearing us groan at the thought of another strip search, he said he'd speak to the officer in the small room and see if it could not be passed over. He returned and said that the officer had to go by procedure. He almost apologized. At least he shrugged and said he'd pick us up after the visit. He left smiling.

Two by two we were invited into the small room and told to strip it all off. A wooden shelf on one wall was divided into little boxes to hold any personal belongings. We had none, but other inmates had left cigarettes, watches, matchbooks, and combs there. I was tiring of stripping so often. And to go through the ritual in a small room was not making me very high. In fact, I caught for the first time an awareness of humiliation. The damned ceremony works, after all, I thought. But all of us were in and out and finally led through the large visiting room, one hack at the desk on duty. Paintings by prisoners hung on the walls, the ceiling was high, the windows arched, and again the Old English Hall came back to me and I felt burdened by all this property cementing me in. We flowed down the corridor leading to that visiting room from the front desk where two hacks met visitors and arranged over phones for the inmates to come down from their cells or dormitories. And there in a room beside the main desk, we were welcomed by Joe Rogers, the gentle Quaker, and other draft violators, Selective Service fuck ups. Phil Berrigan had not arrived yet, but he was due.

I was anxious to meet Phil Berrigan, whom I had known of but had never met during the five or six years of my Peace Movement involvement. We had published articles in the same issue of the *Worker* on several occasions. So I felt close to him. He had a command of words, a tone to his rhetoric that I admired. There was to it a union of emotion and intellect, a kind of meditative rage; an unending series of images as rich as the "Lady with the Unicorn" tapestries; of phrases turned with the wit of John Donne; and emotions as deep as the tradition of enthusiastic religion is long—that stream of mystics, movers, and monks worthy of the name—all flowing in long yet well-carved sentences, forming paragraphs as heavy as foundation stones; the cathedral of his emotions and thought was aspiring; so like the medieval sermons of an Eckhart, so like the kind of meditations Donne was into, so close to the core of me. Compound that contemplative character of his speech and thought with the decisiveness and pragmatic realism of an officer, say, in some freaked-out Children's Crusade, which is the Peace Movement viewed historico-poetically perhaps, and you have Phil Berrigan.

I had heard that he had read some of my articles to men at Allenwood on his work crew when he was in and I was out of jail. He never ceased to organize.

He and his brother Dan Berrigan had been active as co-sponsors and super-stars of that group in the Peace Movement I had first entered. I first met Dan Berrigan, I think, at a sit-in at the United States Mission, across from the U.N. building in New York City. We blocked for a time the same side door of the building, our backs up against the glass doors behind which U.S. marshals would sneer, snarl, and periodically push in an attempt to dislodge us. All the while we were being sung at by women, whom Dan always attracted. When I left that part of the Peace Movement for the *Worker*, I left the circle of people whom Dan and, I suppose, Phil, largely influenced. Dan would show up for a liturgy in one of our apartments near the Bowery. After a while we decided we didn't need a priest to do a liturgy. A little later we decided we did not need the liturgy. By that time underground masses and liturgies were commonplace, indeed fashionable, among liberals in suburbia. We settled in the end for the soup line, our ten o'clock mass.

Our movement of the morning had ceased. The room we were in had cigarette and candy machines in it, and it was not long before a pack of Camels was being passed around and then a second pack. It was not as much fun as doing it when prohibited. There is such a joy to breaking laws. It was news of other lawbreakers in other joints that Joe Rogers provided, as well as bringing in all the underground newspapers and Movement journals that were denied us by prison officials. He had been at the demonstration outside the Allenwood gate, but he had not seen our little frolic on the hillside. He had also gone with the crowd to the Wall of this prison and shouted "Freedom" and heard the reply. Bob was asking him to contact his lawyer by phone tomorrow and get him to press hard on the conditions in segregation. Joe Rogers also had news for David and Jerry. Both of their lawyers had been contacted and they were looking into a recent Supreme Court decision that might get them released. We had words of greeting for the guys at Allenwood whom he would see that afternoon. There was much to read and much to be heard and too much to say.

"Hey, Hobbit," David said, as he stood quietly by the window. "Come, dig this garden."

"Wow, I thought I caught a glimpse of a garden coming into this room, but I dismissed the idea."

"Look, it goes all the way up. There's sky up there."

"An inner courtyard with garden in this Old English Hall."

"What kind of tree is that, Hobbit? That tall, thin one that looks like a candle growing out of that rock."

"How would I know, David. It's a tree. I agree with Dylan Thomas, who said 'All trees are oaks, except fir trees,' and he said about birds, 'All birds are robins, except crows, or rooks.'"

"You aren't very helpful, Hobbit," David said. "You ever check out that tree behind the weight room? It's a high rise apartment—just full of homes. At the top in one of the holes Jerry put one of the American flags he ripped off the graves in the cemetery. All sorts of stuff stashed in that tree besides birds. Look, there's a path to walk."

"Try it and they'll throw you in the 'hole.'"

"Why do they keep such good care of it? Look, all those little hedges are trimmed and those blue and yellow flowers all in a row."

"Obviously, for the same reason it is where it is. Right behind the hack as the visitors approach him from the outside. They can look at the garden the way our visitors can look at our valley and mountain and rest easy. Nothing painful can go down amid such beauty."

The Hole / 184

"Beauty in the hands of the ugly," David said. "You like gardens, Hobbit?"

"To walk in, to smoke a pipe in, yes. But I've never been in the kind of garden I really like."

"What's that, Hobbit?"

"A Japanese or Chinese garden. They really know what Nature is all about. They don't mess with it as much as the English do. Those absurd rational gardens of the English. That's what this one is based on. Nature isn't rational. She isn't that limited. The Oriental may construct or design a garden; but in the end it looks as if Nature had on a holiday adorned herself."

"What's that clanking, grinding sound?" David asked.

"I bet it's the front gate. All the doors are open. Hear it? Like thunder. I came through there once on a visit. I was uptight as hell."

"Why?"

"I was with two women I loved. One was the wife of a friend of mine in here at that time. A C.O. And the other. Well, the other was more beauty and pain than I could handle. Than she could handle. We came from the *Worker* by bus. Drank blackberry brandy on the bus. Only way to do a Greyhound. Well, I thought she still had the brandy in her bag and I was uptight because I knew we'd be searched. So we got inside the first barred gate and were looking at the other. Caged. With a hack looking down on us. Like the tiger cages in Vietnam."

"Well, what happened?"

"Nothing. We were not allowed the visit because we—the pain-crossed beautiful woman and I—were not related to the inmate. His wife alone visited. How blind these officials are. Surely, he was and he is my brother."

"Such thunder, Hobbit. It's like Mordor. There's an evil eye about."

"Yeah, Davy, where you find brick and mortar so structured, so defended, there you will always—cannot be otherwise—find an evil eye."

"Look who came in with the thunder," David said.

"That, indeed, is Philip Berrigan."

The Hole / 185

And I immediately remembered his saying in that article next to mine: "As Pope John used to say, 'Love ought to be the motive, but justice the object.'" Yes, so much a priest. But a different kind of power here. Not the power of authority backed up by tradition, not the power of arbitrary rule, not the power that seeks to subject psyches, not the power that idolizes power. Not the power of priests or statesmen. Truly, here is the power of the great. He seems to be moving, yet he's standing still. All the others clinging to him. He would move through them. He has work to do. It is all over his face. There is little one can do in here, methinks. Little that would satisfy that urge, anyway. And were he to put all that energy to work, it would bring the walls down on his head. He has done things. They too are in his face. Left a lot of energy at Catonsville and carried the word to small Christian tables in suburbia. Yes, the old Emmaus trip: "O Fools and slow of heart," he said to his own disciples. Good that he can do it. Organize the clergy and the nuns. How did I put it in that article next to his about the fast at the Immaculate Conception Shrine? The National Shrine—strange bedfellows there, the Nation and the Shrine. What was it about the one priest and the one nun who showed up to join us—oh, yes, ". . . beautiful mavericks from that huge black herd of clergy and nuns, roaming those environs." Takes a super-cowboy to lasso those mavericks out of that herd. Well, there he is. Let us meet him.

And I wormed my way through the admirers and found him now sitting, yet still surging. The hair was gray, an iron gray. Yes, there was metal there. A helmet. On such a head. Large, heavy workingman features. Give him a hammer. Put him to work on these walls. But those eyes. As bright blue as the flowers David pointed to. And they penetrate.

"Phil Berrigan, I am Jack Cook. It has been a long time," I said, aware of all the raps going down around us.

Our eyes met and locked and his eyes sparkled blue and the sun seemed suddenly to shine on his face, so bright and alive it was. Peace in his eyes, his huge body at rest. So our mountain in a blue haze of noon.

"What brings you to the 'hole'?" he asked, aware too of the raps and the noise.

"We did a little anarchist's walk up a hill. A sort of symbolic escape. It was fun. It got us here."

He smiled and I felt my face smiling. All the muscles of my face seemed on their way to my eyes. It was good. But there were others. On our left, on our right. All, as I, had too much to say. I went back to David by the window. I did not know how Phil would regard such an action as ours. He would have beamed had I said I ripped off a draft board between counts at night and returned to jail with the perfect alibi. But I didn't say that, didn't offer it. Instead, I offered the Walk, the kind of futile Folly *Catholic Workers* are infamous for in the eyes of the more "politically minded." As futile as putting in front of a Bowery man every day a small bowl of soup. As futile as giving out for the third time in one winter day an overcoat to the same Bowery man, whom you know just went around the corner to Louis' Pawn Shop and sold the one you gave him a half hour ago. For a quarter. He needed his wine. But you do it anyway, until the coats run out; because you have no right to tell him how to wear his coat or what to do with his coat. That kind of Folly. That kind of simplicity that lacks for so many any political relevance. Somewhat lacking in externals. With such slender political actions one cannot, I suppose, change the world. But, then, I never ever wished to change that Bowery man.

"Candy, Hobbit. Get some candy," David said.

"Done." And I went over to Joe Rogers and begged some dimes from him and offered the machine its proper sacrifice and it dispensed its blessings in the form of Baby Ruth and Milky Way and Three Musketeers and we feasted on brotherhood and chivalry and sportsmanship under a shining host of stars.

"Hey, come see the hippie-longhair visitors," Alex said from the doorway.

We went over and indeed, in front of the hack's desk, two hippies stood, their faces showing frustration.

"They've been there awhile," Jerry said.

"Can't get their visit, I guess," John said.

"Throw them the peace sign, Alex," David said.

The Hole / 187

And he did.

"What's that gonna get ya?" was the angry reply.

"Wow, did you hear that?" Alex cried. He was hurt.

"Throw him the bird instead," I said.

And the frustration of the two young hippies had found an outlet other than hacks. Their lips almost visibly curled.

"Can't they see we're hippie-longhairs, too?" Jerry asked.

"You're just a con to them," David said.

"We're all just cons," John said.

"Probably in to visit some druggie," I said.

Alex was trying to explain to the young guy that he wasn't after anything, but he had to do it and not disturb the hack just a few feet away. But the young guy seemed too deep into the hassle of the visit. We heard him say he was her, the other long-hair's, husband and it was her brother they wanted to visit. But the hack would only let her visit, not him. Finally, as the hack turned his back on them to search in the file cabinet, Alex was able to connect and get his problem straightened out. We were identified as peace-niks and smiles, a little sad, showed up on their faces. They would not visit split up and asked that that message be conveyed to her brother. They would write for special permission for the hippie-longhair, and then, perhaps, they might visit someone in that largely empty visiting room. They waved and gave us the peace sign as they left.

And I felt guilty about suggesting "the bird" earlier. Always there is an error. A bird should not fly into the sun. It should light on a limb of some huge tree that has a feeder on it that is well fed by the people in the nearby house. There on the limb let it sing. But if the feeder is not fed, then the cats dwelling in the house will move out into their private hunting ground, like aristocrats of old, and kill the weakened birds, who are dependent upon the feeder and are not dwelling in the house but are victims of the cold winter snows. People, feeder, birds, and cats. A life and death struggle. Not for entertainment only.

After the visit was over, Joe Rogers gathered his file full of good folk on the outside together and left. And the dozen or so cons who remained were taken into the large visiting room and

The Hole / 188

told to wait before the door leading into the small room where we would be stripped and searched again.

Sitting there with David and Jerry, John and Alex, Bob and Dickey (whose mother had visited him that day, so he missed the group visit), and Phil and two or three other C.O.'s, as well as one of the other men involved in the Catonsville affair, whom I did not know, we had a chance to talk shop—jailtalk, that is. For Phil was anxious to get out to Allenwood, where the possibilities for action were greater than at Lewisburg.

The room held memories for me and part of my mind focused on them. During my first two weeks in Lewisburg, my wife had visited me in this very room. She was sitting under that long high arched window in the red brick wall. When I came out of the small room after being stripped and searched, feeling uncomfortable in blues that did not fit and aware that my head had been butchered by the barber the day before, I came out into a darkened area and walked slowly into the wider space of this large room. But at that point I did not see my wife. At that point I was blinded by the sun coming through that long high arched window. Its whole long length was bright with light and my eyes were on fire and I could not see my wife and, dazed, I looked around, and, bewildered, I turned in search for her, until gradually my eyes adjusted and she rose, as it were, under the white flame of that window, her blond hair glowing, her smile so soft and sad.

Phil and I agreed that he should play it close if he were to make the move to Allenwood a reality. I suggested that perhaps we had thrown a wrench into his works at least by doing what we did. The administration might not want to compound their problems out at Allenwood.

"What are you into out there?" he asked me.

"I jail with bank robbers, thieves, and torpedoes," I said.

It became clear to me that his mind was on Washington, on foreign policy, on the war and how to stop it, on draft boards and how to rip them off.

"You'll have a problem with Engle if you get to Allenwood," I told him.

"Why is that?"

"Because he is a small man; he has a small man's complex among others. A veritable waldorf salad of sicknesses. He's the type who, when you enter his office, demands that you sit down so he can stand up. Especially with tall men—he hates men bigger than he. He'll be a problem to you."

"What are the others doing? Is there a chance to come together out there?" he said.

"We have our share of quarterbacks. I don't know. We did this thing, but it was a struggle. Everyone seems to be doing his own time. I'm personally opposed to organizing or actions that are going to create more of a wedge between us and other prisoners. I'd rather jail with the hard core than do peace things with C.O.'s."

"Yes, but there is the war and the Movement," he said.

"I've done my little thing for the war. I'm in here. In here I work as I can with the men around me."

"What do you do out there?"

"I teach. Just about run the bloody school. And it's good. I run it as a hustle. Everyone's welcome to sign up. I refuse to take attendance. Get a hack to do it if they want it done. So a lot of guys don't show up for classes. They sack out. But they get out of work. And that is good. I like being used. The others who do show up want to learn. And I can teach them."

"Yes, there is much work to be done in here," he said.

"Are you allowed to say mass?" I asked.

"Yes, but only by myself. I cannot hear confessions, though."

"That might be a good thing in here," I suggested.

"Why is that?" he asked.

"Because it is not good to know too much. There are too many rats and finks around," I said.

"You sound like the hard core," he said.

"I do. And I learned it from them. They are the jailwise."

On the walls around us hung paintings by prisoners. There was a portrait of Mrs. Martin Luther King and several of clowns. There was one in a darkened space of a clown that I could barely distinguish. So I made it into the clown of Rouault. The young clown. I seemed to remember him young, anyway. Part of the side of his head was gone, his eyes were like headlights, the pupils reflected the abyss already. Then he became that other clown, the "Head of a Clown" by Rouault—barely distinguishable behind, underneath the variegations of incredible colors in conflicting shades and fragmented shapes—the polychromatic face of despair. And then he became the other "Head of a Clown," the profile of bitterness, capped, and framed by an arched window, his suspicious eye keeping the viewer at a distance, his mouth an angry tear in a long hard face. Yes, and then he became "The Old Clown," so sad and heavy in the eyes, his lips folded in mute helplessness. And then the old man took on flesh in the face until it was quite round, lips a rich red, his eyes no longer sad but arrogant, stupid; the hate in his eyes backed up by the power of the courts drove his face forward. And suddenly I was looking at "Three Judges," brutal the first, arrogant the second, the contours of legality and justice compromised and caricatured the third. Then the scene was changed once more and "Christ and the Apostles" appeared, silently, their eyes unseeing, downward, inward, quietly at peace together. And that, too, changed and a rounder arch appeared again, and again the profile but a profile reversed and no longer a clown but the "Christ Head" bent with eyes closed, all the dark lines revolving in round white pain suffered in peace and profound nobility. And the circle expanded, the arch disappeared, a figure emerged, naked in repose, silent before the mocking faces.

"Okay, men," a hack said as he came around the corner quickly, "we're going to do this all at once. Save time."

And he knocked on the small window in the door that had not glass but a piece of wood covering it, like a speakeasy door, and the hack inside opened it and our way was opened into the small room and beyond it into the narrow corridor. There we were told to strip and they did and it angered me. And I did not strip until the hack came up and ordered me to and another hack was working on the others.

They were going by a list. When a man's name came up, the hack would go to where he stood naked and do the ritual.

"Hands up and open. Open your mouth. Run your hands through your hair. Lift your balls. Turn around. Bend over. Spread those cheeks. Lift your feet."

The Hole / 191

David's name. John's name. Jerry, Dickey, Bob, and Alex. The others.

"Why so stern a face, Hobbit?" David asked.

"I'm sick of being humiliated. I'm sick of seeing men humiliated."

"Cool it, Hobbit. You'll burn up."

Phil's name. And the expression on the hack's face.